New Life Book Company

Proudly Presents

"The Game of Life"

by Z. Z. Le Mans © 2024

For Lady, The One, The Professor, and
the promise I made in the Dome of Destiny

PARTNERS IN CRIME

Z. Z. Le Mans here. That's me on the right. Behind me and to the left is my cat Lady Le Mans. Lady and I have been partners in crime for the past 19 years and for the past five years have been *homeless* and living in *"The Black Bat"* my ghostly super modified 1966 Corvair. Like Bonnie & Clyde we do what we gotta do to survive in this cruel world. And like Bonnie & Clyde they'll never take us alive.

This is our story . . .

2

VACANT LOT BASEBALL

I was born and raised in the "Monta Vista" section of Cupertino, California in the bygone days when Monta Vista was a poor blue-collar neighborhood dotted fruit orchards and vacant lots where all the poor Monta Vista kids played vacant lot baseball after school.

I was a pretty good ballplayer in those days and once led the vacant lot league in home runs. And each and every Saturday morning I watched Tony Kubek and Joe Garagiola call *The NBC Game of the Week* on channel 4.

3

Tony Kubek & Joe Garagiola

Baseball is more than a game.
It's like life played out on a field.
- Juliana Hatfield

EXPELLED

I was a different kind of kid from the get go and was expelled from Catholic catechism at age eight.

SISTER MARGARET. God created the Heavens and the Earth in six days and rested on the seventh.

I raised my hand.

SISTER MARGARET. Yes, Z.

ME. Sister Margaret, last week you said God was all-powerful.

SISTER MARGARET. Yes, that's right, Z. God is all-powerful.

ME. Then why does he need to *rest???*

Everyone laughed except Sister Margaret.

One Year Later . . .

SISTER MARGARET. When you accept our Lord Jesus Christ as your "Savior" Jesus removes all your sins and makes you clean and whole again.

I raised my hand.

SISTER MARGARET. Yes, Z.

ME. Sister Margaret, how does Jesus remove our sins??? Does he put our sins in a brown paper lunch bag and then toss the bag into a dumpster or *what?*

My classmates laughed again.

Suffice it to say Sister Margaret and the parish priest came to regard me as a heretic and a bad influence on the other students and so I was *expelled* from Catholic catechism.

PRAISE GOD ! ! !

I wasn't an *atheist.* Far from it. I believed in God or some incomprehensible *Higher Power* at work in the Universe, but I had a deep *inner knowing* that the Catholic Church had it all *wrong. Where* this deep *inner knowing* came from I had no clue, but that would be revealed to me decades later in *The Dome of Destiny.*

The Catholic Church believes in a God that needs to *rest.* The idea that God needs to rest is ludicrous and an *insult* to God.

ARCHANGEL MICHAEL. God! Come quick! We need your help! A Black Hole is about to swallow up nebula 176.295.932-7A.

GOD. I'm tired and my back's out. Addios nebula 176.295.932-7A. It was nice knowin' ya.

Fast Forward 7 years.

Despite being expelled from Catholic catechism my mother insisted I attend Catholic mass on Christmas and Easter. But by age 15 I had enough Catholic bullshit for one lifetime and decided to take a stand . . .

BANG!!! BANG!!! BANG!!!

That's my brainless stock clerk mother (BSCM) banging on my door.

BSCM. Get dressed Z! We're late for Easter mass!

ME. I'm not going.

BSCM. *What???*

ME. I'm not going.

BSCM. Whataya mean you're not going???

ME. I'm not going.

BSCM. You *have* to go.

ME. No, I don't.

BSCM. Why don't you wanna go???

ME. The Catholic Church has it all *wrong*.

BSCM. But we're *Catholic*.

ME. *I'm* not.

Long silence as my brainless stock clerk mother attempts to wrap her puny little indoctrinated mind and dogmatic beliefs around the existential, philosophical, ontological, theological challenge I have calmly and defiantly placed at the temple of her ignorance.

Then, in a voice laden with shock, surprise, defeat, confusion, bewilderment, and utter incomprehension, my brainless stock clerk mother replied,

BSCM. Well...*alright*...if that's how you *feel.*

That morning little 15-year-old Z. Z. Le Mans owned his Scorpio powers, grew balls of steel, stood up to his mother, rejected centuries of Catholic lies and misinformation, and in so doing freed his mind, body, soul, and spirit from the shackles, chains, and tyranny of the Catholic Church forever.

PRAISE GOD ! ! !

HIGH SCHOOL

Growing up in Monta Vista I naturally attended *Monta Vista High School* where I was a fringe member of the stoner clique all four years. I say fringe member because I was the only member of the stoner clique who didn't smoke weed. What bonded the stoner clique and I together was our mutual love of *Classic Rock*. I was a decent self-taught guitarist by then and entertained everyone by playing famous licks and riffs on my guitar which I often brought to school.

The stoners were glad to have me on board for entertainment value, but found me a bit *odd* because I didn't smoke weed and seemed *obsessed* with the BIG questions of LIFE.

Questions Like

Why are we here?

What is the meaning of life?

Is there a God?

Why is there evil in the world?

Is there life after death?

Do bad people go to Hell?

Is Heaven real?

Have we lived before?

Is there life on other planets?

To my shock and amazement *none* of my stoner friends were remotely interested in *any* of these questions and were only interested in bands, girls, cars, and weed.

My psychology and priorities were so different from my high school peers that they often joked I was from another planet.

On top of that I'm a *Scorpio* and for the past 4,000 years the greatest minds in history have tried to fathom the infinite mystery of the Scorpio *personality* and have failed miserably.

PHIL WOOD & COMPANY

After high school graduation the members of the stoner clique scattered to the four winds and I took a job as a robotics programmer at Phil Wood & Company and was trained by the great Phil Wood himself, the eccentric genius creator of radical bicycle part designs famous throughout the world.

Despite great pay and a great boss, working in *Robotics* didn't exactly "do it" for me and after a year I began to dread coming to work. Conversely, Phil Wood was the *happiest* man in the world.

"Phil, you're the *happiest* man in the world. What's your *secret???*" I asked.

Without hesitation Phil replied, "I *love* what I do. The secret to *happiness* is *love* what you do."

"*Hmmm,*" I mused, "Then I guess I *don't* love Robotics."

"Then you have to find what you love and <u>DO IT</u>, or you will be miserable your entire life as so many people are."

This was some Yoda level advice Phil was giving me and I took it to heart. I resigned from the company two weeks later with Phil's blessing, warm handshake, and best wishes.

There aren't many Phil Woods in this world, and this world *desperately* needs more Phil Woods.

THE UPSTART CROW INCIDENT

I was now unemployed and completely uncertain about my next move in life. Feeling restless and confused, I decided to visit a local bookstore called *"The Upstart Crow."* I wasn't there to buy a book. I wasn't there to look at books. I didn't even like books. I merely hoped a change in scenery would clear my mind and give me a clue about my next move in life.

But the two hours I spent roaming *"The Upstart Crow"* was no help at all and I still hadn't the foggiest clue what my next move in life should be. Feeling confused and defeated I began to walk toward the exit . . .

When the student is ready
the master appears.

- Buddhist Proverb

Just then an invisible *Force* gently (but firmly) took hold of me and began to steer my body this way and that way through the bookstore.

I was in *shock*, but this *Force* (whatever it was) immediately sent me a telepathic message, *"Don't be afraid. I'm taking you to a book."*

The voice was male, strong, clear, and *infinitely* wise. *Who* or *What* this male spirit was I had no clue, but I felt in supremely good hands and followed his lead without reservation.

The spirit led me to a particular book on a particular shelf. When I read the title of the book I got vertigo and almost fell over.

The book was . . .

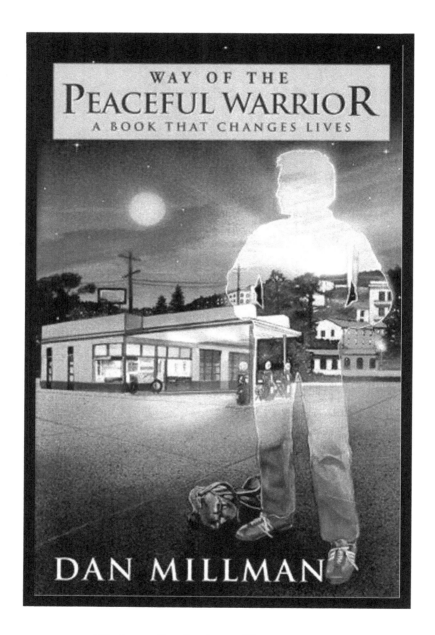

WAY OF THE
PEACEFUL WARRIOR
A BOOK THAT CHANGES LIVES

DAN MILLMAN

That was the day I met *The Professor*.

I MEET THE BUDDHA

WAY of the PEACEFUL WARRIOR inspired me to study Buddhism. Not one to beat around the bush or study with incompetent fools I knocked on Buddha's door.

Knock. Knock. Knock.

The door opened.

BUDDHA. Greetings grasshopper. How can I help you?

ME. Greetings Master. If you please, I have a few questions about *Life* and *Buddhism*.

BUDDHA. No problem. I'm having a sale this week. $10 per question.

ME. *Huh???*

BUDDHA. Just kidding. What are your questions?

ME. Master, what is the purpose of life?

BUDDHA. Self-Improvement.

ME. And what is the purpose of *Buddhism?*

BUDDHA. Self-Improvement.

ME. Master, how do Buddhists deal with the problem of *sin?*

BUDDHA. There is no sin in Buddhism.

ME. No *sin???*

BUDDHA. No. What other religions call "Sin" we call *mistakes.*

ME. That's *interesting*. So, how do Buddhists deal with the problem of *mistakes?*

BUDDHA. We teach to *learn* from your mistakes and do *better* next time.

ME. That's *it???*

BUDDHA. And *meditate.*

ME. Yeah, I heard about this *meditation* business. What's that all *about???*

BUDDHA. Meditation *clears* the mind so you can do better next time.

ME. I begin to see how *everything* in Buddhism relates to *Self-Improvement.*

BUDDHA. You learn *fast* grasshopper.

ME. Master, what happens when we die?

BUDDHA. When the body dies the soul returns to the *Spirit World* and receives a 3D holographic life review.

ME. What is the *purpose* of this 3D holographic life review?

BUDDHA. The purpose of the 3D holographic life review is to see the *mistakes* you made in life so you can do better next time.

ME. *Next time???*

BUDDHA. In your next life.

ME. *Ahhhh,* so Buddhists believe in *reincarnation,* is that it?

Buddha chuckled.

BUDDHA. Reincarnation is not a *belief* grasshopper; it is a *reality.*

ME. Thank you, Master. You have given me a great deal to think about.

BUDDHA. You are an very earnest young man, grasshopper.

ME. Yes, Master; from an early age I felt I had a great mission in life.

BUDDHA. Then you have a great mission in life.

ME. But Master, how shall I know the details of my mission?

BUDDHA. Fear not grasshopper; the gods will guide you; they always do.

ME. Thank you, Master. I have no more questions.

BUDDHA. Then go grasshopper and be brave, for the *Path of Truth* is the most difficult path of all, and you will encounter critics, saboteurs, naysayers, and cutthroats who oppose the *Truth* and all who bring forth the *Truth.* May the gods guide and protect you grasshopper.

And with that, Buddha smiled, flashed a peace sign, and closed the door.

DE ANZA COLLEGE

Thereafter, I devoted my life to endless "self-improvement" which began with a three year stint at De Anza College.

During my three year tenure at De Anza College I was a *key* player in the Theater Dept., Philosophy Dept., and school newspaper. I won leading roles in all the college plays, won a California State writing award for my work on the school newspaper, and penned *"The greatest philosophy term paper in the history of De Anza College"* according to Dr. Vician, Head of the Philosophy Dept., who said I should become a philosophy professor. But I had other plans; my dream was to be a Hollywood actor and screenwriter*!*

So, at the end of my three year stint at De Anza College I loaded up my clunker college car with my scant worldly possessions and drove to Hollywood with only $400 in my pocket and BIG dreams in my head.

SHATTERED DREAMS

I arrived in Hollywood late due to some car trouble and checked into a cheap sleazy downtown motel right off Hollywood Blvd.

To wind down from the long stressful drive I decided to take a stroll along Hollywood Blvd. and do some Hollywood sightseeing. I walked along Hollywood Blvd. and took in all the famous names in stars and was *literally* living the lyrics to *"Celluloid Heroes"* by The Kinks . . .

"You can see all the stars as you walk down Hollywood Boulevard. Some that you recognize. Some that you've hardly even heard of. People who worked and suffered and struggled for fame. Some who succeeded and some who suffered in vain."

It was fun. I was having a blast. I felt on top of the world. I was sure I would succeed in Hollywood. Suddenly, I received a telepathic warning from The Professor regarding a sketchy young black man walking in the opposite direction along Hollywood Blvd. The Professor's warning was vague, but seemed to be something along the lines of *"Watch out for this guy."* I looked the young man over, but despite his sketchy appearance I didn't see any real danger. If he started a fight I could probably take him, but as he drew near he said nothing to me and it seemed like we would pass without incident. But when we got side-by-side he quickly sucker punched me in the head as hard as he could and I fell hard on the sidewalk. I was now fully disabled and barely conscious. I thought he might lay into me some more as I lay there defenseless on the ground but to my surprise he just kept on walking.

I was treated at *Hollywood Presbyterian Hospital* and given bad news. I had two skull fractures, a fractured cheek bone, and a 1-inch cut under my left eye which would require stitches, and a throbbing concussion.

I couldn't believe it. I had only been in Hollywood for four hours and already my Hollywood dreams had gone up in smoke ! ! !

I returned home for a long and painful four month recovery. The incident had a profoundly negative effect on me and thereafter I had NO desire to return to Hollywood ever again.

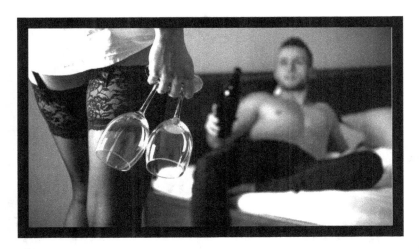

I FALL INTO ADDICTION

After the DEATH of my Hollywood dream I supported myself with a long series of meaningless *unfulfilling* jobs that left me depressed, miserable, melancholy, and I soon sought relief from my pain in a smoky haze of sex, alcohol, and cigarettes. And before long I was heavily *addicted* to all three.

The next ten years of my life were lost to addiction and during those years my creative output as a writer, actor, and musician was ZERO. I literally flushed ALL my talent down the toilet in favor of a cocktail of sex, alcohol, and cigarettes that left me feeling *numb* and *half alive* for ten years.

During those ten years I didn't see or hear from *The Professor* at all and I began to think that maybe I had only imagined *The Professor* and that he really didn't exist.

I sent my soul through the invisible, some letter of that Afterlife to spell, and by and by my soul returned to me and answered, "I myself am Heaven and Hell."

Omar Khayyam

A STRANGE ENCOUNTER

The summer of 2004 was the apex of my addiction years and one day in the summer of 2004 I came home with a big bag of beer, wine, and cigarettes in preparation for another week of dubious *self-therapy*. As I reached for my keys to unlock the door to my cottage I noticed an exquisitely colored gray cat sitting atop my tool shed as if she were the *Egyptian Sphinx*.

I hated cats my entire life because when I was five years old my friend's cat scratched my face for no reason and the incident left a lasting scar on my psyche. Thereafter, cats were my sworn enemy and whenever I saw a cat I would chase it off. But the encounter with *this* cat was different and the cat elicited three feelings in me *simultaneously* . . .

1) I felt no desire to chase the cat off, which was weird.

2) I had the strange feeling the cat liked me, which was really weird.

3) And I had the bizarre feeling that I liked the cat, which was freaky ass weird.

The cat had deep green *kaleidoscope* eyes and had me under some strange *hypnotic* spell with her steady piercing gaze. I was frozen in place and couldn't move. Then the strangest thing happened. The cat spoke to me *telepathically* . . .

"Hello, Mr. Man."

WTF??? The feeling was *otherworldly.* I suddenly felt dizzy, off-balance, and my body began to sway gently like a palm tree in the wind. Something very strange was happening between me and this cat and I just couldn't be in the presence of this mysterious cat anymore. And so I walked into my cottage, lied down on my bed, closed my eyes, and tried to forget what had just happened. I then fell into a very relaxing quasi sleep for 30 minutes after which I rose from my bed and sheepishly looked out the window to see if the cat was still there. *The cat was gone and I breathed a sigh of relief.*

A week later I returned from the store and froze in my tracks. The same mysterious cat was perched atop my blue recycling bin. The sight of the cat unnerved me again, but not as much as the first time.

"Hello Mr. Man."

The cat had the voice of a little girl.

After saying "Hello" the cat just gazed at me placidly and I gazed back. We just stood there gazing at each other for a while, not in an awkward way, but in a warm friendly way. The cat clearly liked me and wanted to be *friends*. This was a *first* because cats usually sense that I don't like them and run away.

Nevertheless, I still felt awkward and queasy about this whole *cat* situation. It didn't make sense. And it put me in a psychological *funk* that didn't feel good. And there were so many unanswered questions. *Who did this cat belong to??? Was it a stray cat??? Why was the cat coming to me??? Why was I into this cat when I don't like cats???*

This cat was a riddle wrapped in a mystery inside an enigma. Well, at the moment I didn't have time for *riddles*—or *cats!* I was in the middle of opening my parapsychology practice and still had tons of work to do. So, I waved goodbye to the cat and walked into my cottage to resume work.

Thereafter, the cat returned every few days—*usually appearing out of nowhere*—or so it seemed. And little by little, visit by visit, the cat and I became better acquainted. And after a few weeks of playing "<u>Now You See Me, Now You Don't</u>" the cat began to rub up against my leg and purr affectionately! To my shock and amazement I bent down and pet the cat while my mind screamed, *What the hell are you doing!!! You're petting a cat!!!*

None of this made any sense. I hate cats. I mean, I used to. And there were plenty of "*Cat Lovers*" in the neighborhood. *Why* was she coming *me???*

After a few minutes of petting and purring I stood up and the cat quietly sashayed off into the distance and out of sight. What a *strange* cat. As time marched on I began to look forward to these random encounters with the mysterious cat.

Thereafter, I didn't see the cat for *two* weeks and when I did she looked *thinner*. I concluded she was a stray cat and wasn't finding much food, so I decided to feed her. All I had on hand was a bag of potato chips and so I pulled a potato chip from the bag and held in front of her mouth. She stared at the potato chip *quizzically* (as if to say, "What the fuck is *this???*"), licked the potato chip tentatively, made a sour face, and gently turned her head away. I got the *message*. Potato chips *aren't* her thing. Then she said to me telepathically,

"Don't you have any *cat* food*???*"

Then as a *test* I attempted to answer the cat *telepathically* by simply *thinking* the words in my head and see if it worked.

"No. I don't."

"Isn't there a store around here?"

It worked ! ! !

"Yeah, there's a store right over..." Oh my god! Do you see what she's *doing???* She wants me to go to the store and get her some cat food. But if I go to the store and get her some cat food she'll think I adopted her and I'm her *Daddy!!!*

Okay. *Look.* It didn't want the cat to starve to death, but I also didn't want to be a cat Dad! I knew there were "Cat Lovers" in the neighborhood; where in the hell were they*???* This whole situation was a cat lover's wet dream. C'mon, cat lovers!!! We got a cat in *need* here!!! Step up to the plate and do your cat lover *duties!!! Chop-Chop!!!*

Nothin'. Not a cat lover in sight.

So, I said to the cat, "I'm sorry. That's all the food I have. Don't worry. You're *cute*. Some cat lover is gonna scoop you up and make you their own. Just hang in there . . ."

The cat lowered her head sadly and I walked into my cottage feeling queasy and confused about my relationship with this cat. When I looked out the window 20-minutes later the cat was gone and I felt a mixture of relief and sorrow.

I didn't see the cat for another *two* weeks and when I did she was *deathly* thin and it didn't look like she would live more than a week and her face looked extremely depressed and despondent.

Right then and there something came over me and I made a monumental decision of galactic magnitude that would alter my life *forever . . .*

I looked her square in the eye and said, "Okay listen. Listen to me. Listen *up!* You live here now. You live here *now!* *Understand???* You live *here* now. Don't move. Stay right *there*. Don't go anywhere. I'm going to the store to get you some cat food. I'm going right *now*. I'll be right back. Don't go anywhere."

I returned from the store with a bag of dry cat food and the cat was sitting demurely on the porch like Cleopatra waiting for her man servant to serve lunch on a silver plate.

I opened the bag of dry cat food, poured some into a bowl, and placed the bowl in front of the cat. Her razor sharp fangs attacked the dry cat food like a ravenous shark. But after just a few bites the cat abruptly stopped and looked at me disappointed.

"What's *wrong???*" I asked.

"I prefer *canned* cat food," she said.

"You prefer *canned* cat food?"

"Yeah."

"Why didn't you tell me?"

"You didn't ask."

The cat was starving, but still finicky, and I was now getting a crash course in "Cat Psychology." So, I went back to the store and returned with some canned cat food, opened a can, and placed the can in front of her. Her razor sharp fangs attacked the food like before, and just like before she abruptly stopped eating after just a few bites and gave me another disappointed look.

"What *now???*" I asked.

"I don't like *this* one."

"You don't *like* this one???"

"No."

"What's *wrong* with *it???*"

"It tastes like *barf*."

"It tastes like *barf???*"

"*Barf* or *poop*; it's hard to tell."

I sighed heavily. Feeding a cat was a lot harder than I thought it would be.

"Alright. Just tell me *exactly* what you want and I'll get some."

"I don't know *exactly* what I want, Mr. Man. Just bring home a dozen different kinds of canned cat food and I'll pick out the *winners*."

"Just bring home a dozen different kinds of canned cat food and you'll pick out the *winners???*"

"Yeah. And you don't have to repeat everything I say."

SASSY ! ! !

I could see this cat was gonna be a handful and I already regretted my decision. It was only our first day together and I already wanted to return her. But return her *where???* Anyway, it was *too* late. I said, "*You live here now.*" I couldn't go back on my word. For better or worse I now had a cat!

I went back to the store and returned with a dozen different kinds of canned cat food and "Miss Finicky" picked out a few cans she liked.

Late that first evening the cat yawned with a full belly and said, "I see you only have only *one* bed, Mr. Man."

"Yeah???"

"Where're you gonna *sleep???*"

"We're gonna be *bunkmates*," I smiled.

Miss Sassy Pants replied, "Mr. Man, in human years I'm a 12-year-old girl. I don't think it would be proper for us to be *bunkmates*. You can sleep on the *floor.*"

WTF ? ? ?

It was time to put Miss Sassy Pants in her place.

"Look here little lady; this here's *my* home, and I'm captain of the ship. So, unless you wanna be homeless *again* we're gonna be bunkmates, *understand???*"

"Well, since you put it that way, Mr. Man, I suppose we could be *bunkmates*—provided you mind your *manners.*"

"I always mind my *manners*. Can you mind *yours???*"

"I'll *try*," she quipped.

At this point I still had no name for this sassy little *lady*, which gave me an idea—I'll call her *Lady*. And maybe the name will remind her she's a *lady* and improve her manners some???

Time will tell . . .

As the days and weeks passed Lady and I quickly developed a fun, zippy, banter-filled relationship and were as happy as could be. I was truly surprised and amazed at how much joy and pleasure this starving stray cat had brought to my life.

Then one day there came three ominous knocks upon the door...

Knock. Knock. Knock.

I opened the door and beheld a woman I had never seen before.

"Do you have our cat?" she asked.

"Your cat???" I gasped. "A cat moved in here about six weeks ago. Was that your cat???"

"May I see the cat?"

I called out to Lady and Lady slowly sashayed into the room. Upon seeing the cat the woman said,

"Yes, that's our cat Gracie."

I couldn't argue. I had no idea where Lady came from, so most likely the woman was telling the truth and Lady was her cat. I was heartbroken. I had already become attached to Lady. And now this strange woman was coming to take Lady away forever. Well, there was nothing I could do about it. It was what it was. I pet Lady goodbye and fought back my tears.

What happened next was like the climactic scene in a "Feel Good" movie. Lady wouldn't go with the woman and hid behind my legs ! ! !

An awkward silence befell the room.

"Hmmm. That's interesting," the woman muse. "Gracie seems to like it here better with you."

34

More awkward silence.

"Hmmm. Well, we have *two* other cats. Would you like to keep Gracie???"

I could hardly contain my excitement. "Yes, I would. I will take care of *Gracie* better than I take care of myself. *Gracie* will be in good hands. You have nothing to worry about."

The woman smiled, "Okay then. Gracie is now your cat." And with that the woman left never to be seen ever again.

"Whew. That was a close one, Mr. Man."

"You didn't tell me you were a teenage runaway."

"You didn't ask. Besides, I'm *not* a teenager; I'm 12."

I kept thinking about Lady's former name and it was all I could do to keep from bustin' a gut.

"*Gracie???*"

"Shut up."

EVICTED

Lady and I enjoyed 14 happy years in that old rustic cottage I rented in Cupertino *(pictured above with Lady walking along my car, something she very often did).*

Then, in late December 2018, Lady and I received an eviction letter from the landlords. The landlords had decided to tear down that old rustic cottage and sell the land to developers. Thus, Lady and I had to move out of the cottage by March 1, 2019.

THE BLACK BAT

At the time of our eviction I had been unemployed for the past two years, during which time I wrote the Pilot and Bible for an original dramatic TV Series titled *"Moscato"* which is loosely based on my career as a *parapsychologist*. The show is named after the main character *Mike Moscato*.

At the time of our eviction *"Moscato"* was still unsold and I had very little money left in the bank. Further, *who* would rent to a man who had been unemployed for the past two years and was *still* unemployed???

I knew the answer to that.

Thus, on March 1, 2019 Lady and I were forced to begin living in *The Black Bat* my super modified 1966 Corvair which has been my ride for the past 30 years!

[AUTHOR'S NOTE, *I aced two years of Auto Shop in high school, am a lifelong 1960's car buff, and for a time was a speed shop machinist at ACTION AUTO MACHINE SHOP in Santa Clara, CA*]

The Black Bat in front of historic "Paul & Eddie's" dive bar, Cupertino, California. My grandfather and his cement plant coworkers often came here for a drink after work in the 1940's and 1950's. Sadly, Cupertino has completely changed since then and today "Paul & Eddie's" is the only landmark left from my childhood.

A ROUGH
FIRST NIGHT

Our first night sleeping in the car was rough—almost impossible.

LADY. Scoot over Mr. Man.

ME. Huh?

LADY. Scoot over.

ME. Huh??? What???

LADY. Scoot your butt over.

ME. Why???

LADY. I can't stretch out my legs.

ME. I can't stretch out my legs either. It's a small car.

LADY. I can't sleep with my legs scrunched up like this. It's uncomfortable.

ME. My legs are scrunched up too.

LADY. But you're a man, Mr. Man. You're tough. You can take it. I'm a little girl. Show some *chivalry.*

I scoot over a little.

ME. There.

LADY. A little more.

I scoot over a little more.

ME. Okay?

LADY. A tad more.

I scoot over a tad more.

LADY. A little *more* . . .

I sigh heavily and scoot over a little more.

LADY. Just a tad more.

I scoot over a tad more.

LADY. That was *half* a tad. Gimme a *whole* tad.

I grunt and scoot over a tad more.

ME. Okay now?

Silence.

ME. Okay now??

Silence.

ME. Okay now???

I look over.

Lady is *asleep.*

Sleeping on the streets was tough, so we decided to relocate to "Blackberry Farm"—a wild nature preserve just a few blocks away.

It was very *dark* and very *quiet* in the Blackberry Farm parking lot. Perfect for sleeping in the car.

Our first night at Blackberry Farm—10:56pm.

"Mr. Man?"

"Yeah?"

"I gotta pee."

"You gotta pee?"

"Yeah. Maybe #2 also."

"Ahhh. Okay. Umm. I'll open the door and you do your kitty business outside and come right back."

"Sounds good."

I opened the driver door and Lady stepped out into the pitch black night.

"Don't go too far. Stay close to the car."

"Yes, Dad," Lady quipped.

I was tired, groggy, and had two mini bottles of chardonnay earlier, the combination of which made me sleepy and I fell asleep at the wheel while Lady was out doing her kitty business.

When I woke up I checked the time on my cellphone and freaked out. It was 12 midnight!!! I was asleep for an hour!!! I quickly rolled down the driver window and called out to Lady.

LADY ! ! ! LADY ! ! !

Nothing. No sight or sound of Lady. Then I jumped out of the car with my flashlight and looked around for Lady. It was pitch black outside and difficult to see even with the flashlight. And to make matters worse it had begun to rain and a strong wind begun to eerily howl. I called out to Lady again and again . . .

LADY ! ! ! LADY ! ! !

No sign of Lady.

The rain and wind suddenly grew much stronger and I realized there was nothing more I could do tonight. The best I could do now was go to bed, get some sleep, and search for Lady in the morning . . .

LADY IS LOST

The next morning I awoke at dawn and searched for Lady for an hour or more. *No sight or sound of Lady.* My heart got heavy and a queasy feeling entered my stomach. This was a *worst* case scenario. Lady was lost in a wild Nature Preserve full of mountain lions, bobcats, rattle snakes, coyotes, and god knows what else. I became consumed with self-loathing and blamed myself for falling asleep at the wheel while Lady was out doing her kitty business. Then I started to panic. *How* am I ever going to find Lady in the *vast* Nature Preserve??? It's *huge.* It will be like searching for a needle in a haystack. My head began to spin and I got vertigo.

At this point in time Lady and I had been together 15 years and were a *Dynamic Duo*. We went together like blue and sky. Together we were *amazing*. Apart we were *nothing*.

So right then and there I felt like *nothing* and I know Lady must be feeling the same way too if—*gulp*—she was still alive!

Some things cannot and should not *ever* be *separated* and Lady and I fall into that rare category. When Lady and I are separated the Universe loses its equilibrium, *Time* and *Space* feel out of phase, and God is nowhere to be found.

With utter dread and anguish I realized that Lady might be lost *forever*—or even worse—*DEAD*.

LIVE

Kim Freeman
THE CAT DETECTIVE

THE CAT DETECTIVE

I searched the Blackberry Farm nature preserve for Lady for five *long* days and nights.

No sign of Lady.

I felt tired, depressed, defeated, and way in over my head. I didn't know how to find a cat and I had no idea what I was doing.

It finally occurred to me that their might be help online so I typed "How to Find a Lost Cat" in the Google search bar and hit ENTER. This popped up . . .

KIM FREEMAN ✦ CAT DETECTIVE
"Professional Lost Cat Finder"
www.lostcatfinder.com

Holy shit!!! I found the Sherlock Holmes of lost cats!!! Kim was in Atlanta Georgia but for a reasonable fee Kim provided me with her 100-Page "Lost Cat" ebook and a little phone assistance.

Sure enough, according to Kim's ebook I was doing everything *wrong* and had literally *wasted* the first five days of my search for Lady. The lost five days were costly. Lady could literally be *miles* away by now in *any* direction. Finding Lady now would be like finding a needle in a haystack.

THE DOOR AJAR TECHNIQUE

Kim suggested we start with what she called "The Door Ajar Technique."

KIM. Park exactly where you lost Lady and sleep with your door ajar six inches. Place some of Lady's favorite food at the foot of the door. This will lure Lady back and into the car.

I thought this was a great idea but had a few reservations.

ME. Sounds good, but the last five nights have been a rainy 37 degrees. I'll probably freeze to death with the door ajar and sleeping all night with an open door in a dark Nature

Preserve is a serial killer's "wet dream," not to mention the mountain lions who regard a man sleeping with his car door open as their all night *"Burger King."*

Long silence on the phone.

I don't think Kim got my sense of humor.

Then, with a tone of admonishment she replied,

KIM. *Well,* do you want your cat *back???*

THE NIGHT WALKER

The 13th day of the search for Lady began ominously with 37 degree freezing rain, a howling wind, and that creepy number 13.

I knew Lady wouldn't come out in this freezing windy rain, but I left the door ajar anyway because that's what I was told to do.

Each night I made every effort to stay awake so that if Lady, a mountain lion, or a serial killer approached I would be ready. However, most nights I fell asleep about 1AM and this night was no different.

Later on, at about 3AM, I was awoken by some strange sounds. I didn't know what the sounds were at first but they were getting closer. As the sounds grew closer it sounded more and more like people talking. My first thought was, *Who would be conversing in this cold rainy Nature Preserve at 3AM???* Only one answer came to mind . . .

Twisted Fuck Serial killers ! ! !

As I wiped the sleep from my eyes and looked around, their conversation grew louder and closer. I instantly went into *"Fight or Flight"* mode but had no weapons other than my bare hands and these twisted fuck serial killers no doubt had guns and knives and I figured I was about to exit this world, but god-damn-it, I was gonna give those Satanic bitches one hell of a fight before they killed me!

Their voices were loud and nearly upon me now. In a moment I would see them. My heart raced. Suddenly, out of the dark cold rainy abyss appeared a man wearing a *black* trench coat, a *black* fedora hat, and holding a *black* umbrella.

He looked like the Angel of Death.

But what happened to the *other* men??? Where did *they* go??? The first man kept right on talking without missing a beat. I then realized to my shock and horror that this twisted fuck *Angel of Death* was all alone and vocalizing all parts of the conversations *himself!!!*

This was beyond creepy. This was creepy on steroids. This was creepy on acid. This was creepy on DMT. This was alternate universe dark matter creepy ass shit from Hell!!!

Yeah, well, I didn't need any creepy ass shit in my life right now; I'm here looking for my cat!!!

Then *something* caught my attention. I suddenly realized I didn't recognize the *language* he was speaking. I'm not even sure it *was* a language. It sounded like he was speaking in *tongues!!!* And *multiple* tongues at that!!!

I WAS TRAPPED IN AN INTERDIMENSIONAL
VORTEX OF WEIRDNESS ! ! !

One thing was sure. He would be on me soon and mortal combat would be imminent. I was prepared to fight to the *death*, but to my shock and amazement he just walked right past me without so much as a glance in my direction.

WTF??? He must have seen me. He must have seen the car. How could he *not* see me*???* I became confused. If he's not a twisted fuck serial killer what the hell is he doing walking in the freezing cold rain in a Nature Preserve at 3AM*???* It didn't make sense. Nothing about this guy made any sense and I felt like I was in the middle of a *"Twilight Zone"* episode.

Well, whatever his motives, he was gone now, and a sense of *relief* washed over me. I tried to go back to sleep and forget the whole thing. But five minutes later I heard his psycho babble approaching again!!!

Nooooooo ! ! !

What is up with this dude??? Why is he *back???* Did he decide to kill me afterall*???* I rose up from my makeshift bed and prepared for mortal battle with this dude, whatever he

53

was. But just like before, The Night Walker passed by without so much as a glance in my direction and disappeared once more into the cold rainy blackness of the Nature Preserve.

What the hell is going on here ? ? ?

I couldn't sleep for fear The Night Walker would return and return he did five minutes later, and the same exact pattern played out again as it had on the two previous encounters. Then I understood what he was doing . . .

He was walking "laps" around the parking lot ! ! !

But why??? What was the point of all this??? I'm here looking for my cat. But what the hell is he doin' here??? Then I had a chilling realization . . .

He's never going away ! ! !

He's gonna walk "laps" around me all night long and that's exactly what he did. The Night Walker walked "laps" around me all night long and then mysteriously disappeared shortly before sunrise.

What the hell was all that about??? To this day I don't know. All I know is he was finally gone, dawn had broken, and I had to keep looking for Lady.

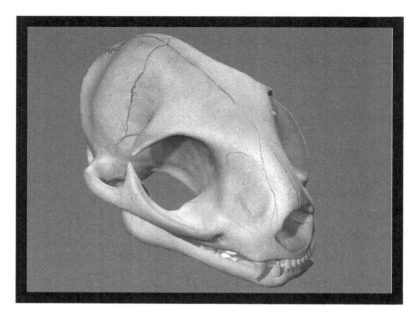

THE CAT SKULL

The next day at 1:22PM I got a phone call from ranger George at Blackberry Farm.

"I have some bad news."

"What?"

"We found a cat skull today."

Nooooooo ! ! !

Ranger George continued, "The skull is about two weeks old. Isn't that about the time you lost Lady?"

It was. The timing was right and my heart sank into my stomach. The thought of Lady being eaten alive by some heartless predator was my worst nightmare. If this cat skull was Lady I would never forgive myself for drinking too much and falling asleep that night. But was it for sure this cat skull was Lady???

Based on the uncanny timing ranger George was convinced the cat skull was my Lady, but I wasn't so sure. My Lady was a scrappy girl and a kickass fighter. Back in the cottage days I watched two racoon bullies attack Lady and Lady had those two racoon bullies running for their lives in seconds*!!!*

No. My gut told me this cat skull wasn't Lady but I had to be sure. I had to inspect the skull myself. A gruesome task but it had to be done, so I asked ranger George, "Can I inspect the skull?"

"Sure. Come to the park museum. I'm there with the skull right now."

When I arrived at the park museum ranger George handed me a brown paper lunch bag and said, "The skull's in here."

Yikes. This was not something I was looking forward to.

My heart pounded hard in my chest as I opened the brown paper bag with utter dread. I pulled out the cat skull with my right hand and got a shock. It was perfectly white and clean.

"Why is it so *white* and *clean?*" I asked.

"Birds, bees, ants, and insects pick it clean in no time," ranger George replied.

This was bad news. I was hoping there would be a tuft of fur on the skull to compare it to Lady's fur. No such luck. Then a thought came to me and I began to *pet* the skull just like I pet Lady.

Ranger George shot me a curious stare.

"I don't think it's Lady," I said.

"What makes you say that?"

"The head doesn't feel right. I know Lady's head like the back of my hand and this doesn't feel like Lady's head."

Ranger George replied, "This is the *only* cat skull we've found in the past six months. I'm sorry, but it *has* to be Lady."

Ranger George was *right*. Everything pointed to this cat skull being *Lady's* skull, but my kickass Scorpio intuition was telling me something else. Then I got an idea.

"May I take the skull to Lady's vet? He has X-rays of Lady's skull and teeth. He should be able to tell for sure."

"That would be fine," replied ranger George. "Just return the skull to the museum when you're done because we want it for our collection."

So, I put the cat skull back into the brown paper lunch bag and drove off to Lady's vet who was just five minutes away.

THE WORST 10 MINUTES OF MY LIFE

Lady's veterinarian (*Dr. Griesshaber*) took the skull out of the paper bag and told me the exam would take about 10 minutes. Those 10 minutes in the waiting room were the worst 10 minutes of my life. Can you imagine waiting 10 minutes to find out if a little white skull in a brown paper lunch bag was your cat!!!

Alone in the waiting room I prayed to God whom I affectionately call *"Big Daddy."*

Dear Big Daddy,

Greetings and Adonai.

Today I find myself in a dire predicament whereby the cat skull Dr. Griesshaber now examines may or may not be the cat skull of my cat Lady.

And so thus then I ask you in the name of all that is holy and wholesome to work your magic powers and make the cat skull which Dr. Griesshaber now examines <u>NOT</u> be Lady's cat skull, but the cat skull of some poor unfortunate cat who is now with You in Heaven.

Big Daddy, if you grant me this request I promise to reduce my drinking to a more reasonable level and not give the middle finger so much when I am driving in town even though half the people on the road deserve the middle finger.

In short Big Daddy, if you grant me this request I will do my utmost (or some reasonable facsimile thereof) to be a better person on this God-forsaken planet.

Thank you and Adonai.

Adonai and Amen.

Just then Dr. Griesshaber returned to the waiting room with the brown lunch bag and a big smile on his face. *"It's not Lady,"* he said.

PRAISE GOD ! ! !

BACK
TO THE CAT
DETECTIVE

The "Door Ajar Technique" was a dismal failure and it was time to call the Cat Detective for further instructions.

ME. The "Door Ajar Technique" isn't working. No sign of Lady. No nothin'.

CAT DETECTIVE. Hmmm. Okay. I don't think she's in the Nature Preserve anymore.

ME. Where do you think she is?

CAT DETECTIVE. She probably decided the Nature Preserve was too dangerous and is now roaming the nearby neighborhood.

ME. Okay. So, what do we do?

CAT DETECTIVE. I'll make you a "Lost Cat Flier" for Lady and email it to you.

ME. Okay? What do I do with that?

CAT DETECTIVE. You mail it to all the people in the neighborhood.

ME. That sounds really expensive. Did you catch the part where I said Lady and I are living in a *car???*

Pregnant silence followed by another dose of admonishment.

CAT DETECTIVE. *Well,* do you want your cat *back???*

JOHN'S IDEA

I received the "Lost Cat Flier" from The Cat Detective and ran the whole idea past my good friend John Freeman (no relation to Kim Freeman, but isn't it *weird* that they're both *Freemans???*)

John said, "I get those Lost Cat fliers in the mail all the time and I throw them in the garbage without even looking at them. No. If you want Lady back tape the fliers over the keyhole of every door in the neighborhood. That way people have to look at Lady's mug shot just to get in their home."

I thought that was a *brilliant* idea and would save me $500 in postage since there would *be* NO postage!!!

A STRANGE DREAM

A few days later I had a strange dream . . .

. . . the dream began with me walking up a San Francisco hill. Cars lined both sides of the street but I didn't see any people. I guess everyone was still sleeping. I continued walking up the hill. Still no sign of people. No pedestrians. No bicyclists. No joggers. And strangest of all, no cars driving on the streets. I got a queasy feeling in the pit of my stomach. Something wasn't right here, but I didn't know what.

I continued walking up the hill when I felt a loud *THUMP* along the ground. What the hell was that??? A moment later it happened again. *THUMP.* And then again. *THUMP.* It seemed to be coming up behind me. I turned around to see what it was and beheld a sight I will never forget. An old wooden telephone pole was "hopping" up the street and directly toward me.

Thump. Thump. Thump.

Weirdest of all, it appeared to be after me! I ran down a side street to see if it would follow me or not.

Thump. Thump. Thump.

It followed me! The damn thing had a mind of its own and was malevolent!

Thump. Thump. Thump.

I ran down another side street, looked over my shoulder, and the goddamn thing was gaining ground!

Thump. Thump. Thump.

I couldn't outrun it!

Thump. Thump. Thump.

I ran down another side street that led straight to a high wooden pier and the San Francisco bay.

Thump. Thump. Thump.

I ran to the end of the pier and the pole closed in on me hard and fast. There was nowhere left to run and so I jumped off the pier and into the San Francisco bay.

The dream ended there.

Time spent
with cats
is never
wasted.

- Sigmund
Freud

FREUD'S COUCH

First thing in the morning I looked for Lady in the nature preserve for an hour but there was still no sign of her, so I drove to a nearby 7-Eleven, bought a cup of coffee, and returned to the nature preserve parking lot to sip my coffee and tried to fathom last night's dream. As I sipped my coffee and gazed at the relaxing green trees and beauty of the nature preserve my mind slowly drifted into a foggy hypnotic daydream and much to my surprise I suddenly found myself on Freud's couch.

"Very inzeresting zream," Freud said in his thick Austrian accent puffing away on his cigar.

"What's your *interpretation* of the dream?" I asked Freud.

Freud gently petted the tiger-striped ginger cat on his desk and said, "I zink zee telephone pole represents jor primal egzistential *fears.*"

"My primal existential *fears???*"

"Jess."

"Could you elaborate on that a little?"

Freud leaned back in his chair, "Zet me ask zu a question. Zu you fear the *danger, hostility,* and *unpredictability* of our *verld?*"

"Yes, *naturally.*"

"Zoes are your primal egzistential fears."

"So, you think the telephone pole represented my primal existential fears?

"Jess."

"But *why* a telephone pole???"

"I zon't know. Maybe jor zubconcious likes zelephone poles," Freud chuckled. "Anyway, the *object* is *irrelevant*; it's *what* the object *does* that madders. In this case, the zelephone pole was hostile and chased you; don't you zee?"

"Yes, I see what you're saying, doctor. The antagonist in the dream could have been *anything*. My subconscious mind simply cast a telephone pole in this movie dream."

"Jess, very vell put."

"But what about the empty streets with no people? What does that *signify???*"

"Zat zignifized jor feeling of being all avone in dis verld vith no vun to help you."

"Whoa, I think you nailed it, doctor."

"Jess, vell, zream interpretation is one of my *specialties*" Freud smiled, cigar smoke floating languidly in the air.

"Dr. Freud, is there any *lesson* in this dream?"

"Jess, a very *profound* lesson."

"What?"

"Stayz away from *San Francisco*."

(We chuckled like father and son. I liked Freud very much. He's a lot cooler than people think.)

"Thank you, doctor. I must travel back to my *Time* now and continue looking for my cat."

"Jess, ju must find jor cat, for cats are better companzions zen people, and time spent with cats is never *vase*-ted."

COYOTES AND MORONS

Blackberry Farm is popular with coyotes and morons and *morons* are by *far* the greater in number.

Something I heard a million times as I searched for my cat Lady was, "Your cat was probably eaten by coyotes," and usually followed by, "It's just a cat. Get another one."

This is like telling the parents of a missing toddler, "Your baby girl was probably torn to shreds by a mountain lion. No big woop. Just have another kid."

Anyway, these asinine coyote comments got me worried so I called The Cat Detective to get her professional opinion.

ME. People are telling me Lady was eaten by *coyotes* ! ! !

CAT DETECTIVE. They always say that.

ME. Well, is it true???

CAT DETECTIVE. I hear the "Coyotes ate your cat" theory all the time and it's a pretty lame theory. For one thing, cats are not very high on a coyote's menu. There are 10 or 12 other animals and rodents coyotes prefer more than cats and a *Nature Preserve* would be full of them.

ME. Okay, that's good news.

CAT DETECTIVE. Moreover, coyotes leave a pile of fur behind because they don't eat the fur. Have you or the rangers discovered a pile of fur that matches Lady's fur???

ME. No.

CAT DETECTIVE. Then Lady has *not* been eaten by coyotes.

That was a load off my mind and a huge relief. I slept better that night knowing that Lady was very likely still alive.

LADY. *Pssst. Pssst.* Gather 'round readers and I'll tell you what happened out there in the woods. Around 3AM a gang of cutthroat ky-otes had me surrounded in a moonlit meadow of the nature preserve. I was there enjoying the beauty of nature and practicing Transcendental Meditation in the stillness of the night when they began lickin' their chops and chattering their teeth. I knew what they were thinkin'. They were thinkin' I was a late night snack. So, I slowly and calmly ejected the five deadly switchblades of my left paw into the moonlight. And then I slowly and calmly ejected the five deadly switchblades of my right paw into the moonlight. That's when FEAR and TERROR washed over the faces of these canine cowards.

COYOTE BOB. Whoa there guys. Hold up. That's *not* a rabbit. That's Lady Le Mans.

COYOTE TIM. You mean the infamous *"Lady of Death???"*

COYOTE SAM. Bob's right. That's no bunny rabbit. That's the *"Lady of Death"* herself.

COYOTE TIM. *"The Lady of Death???"* What you guys talkin' about*???*

COYOTE SAM. You never heard of Lady Le Mans, aka *"The Lady of Death???"*

COYOTE TIM. Nope. I just moved here from the Santa Cruz mountains.

COYOTE SAM. Lady is legendary in these parts.

COYOTE MIKE. Everywhere she goes she leaves a trail of dead ky-otes in her wake, ripped and torn to shreds by her 10 deadly switchblades.

COYOTE DON. That's why we call her *"The Lady of Death."*

COYOTE KEN. According to legend Lady once dismembered a black bear who tangled with her in deez very woods.

COYOTE STEVE. Yeah. My Daddy told me that story too when I was just a wee pup and told me to never tangle with *"The Lady of Death."*

COYOTE DAN. My grampy tangled with *The Lady* back in 2006.

COYOTE JOHN. What happened*???*

COYOTE DAN. Nobody knows. We never saw grampy ever again.

COYOTE JOE. My cousin crossed paths with *"The Lady of Death"* late one night in 2011. We found him in the mornin' torn to shreds. He looked like a plate of spaghetti.

COYOTE TIM. Ok! Ok! I get the picture guys. What do we do *here???*

COYOTE KEN. There's only one thing to do.

COYOTE DAVE. What's that???

COYOTE BUBBA. Abort.

COYOTE SPIKE. *Pssst. Pssst.* Everybody. *Abort. Abort.*

COYOTE KEVIN. (whispering) Full abort mode. Full abort!

COYOTE CURTIS. Back up *fast* but *slow* guys.

COYOTE ED. Sorry Miss Lady. We din't know it 'twas you. We'ez just passin' through lookin' for a little late night snack-a-roo.

COYOTE BILL. We tought you was a bunny rabbit.

COYOTE BOB. Yeah. We tought you was a bunny rabbit.

COYOTE SAM. Our bad Miss Lady. Won't happen again.

COYOTE JIM. Hard to see in deez night woods Miss Lady.

COYOTE CARL. Yeah, you looked like a bunny rabbit.

COYOTE KEVIN. Simple case of mistaken identity *Lady of Death*—I mean Miss Lady.

COYOTE PAUL. No harm no foul Miss Lady.

COYOTE CHRIS. It's all good Miss Lady.

COYOTE TREVOR. We'll just be on our way now.

COYOTE GEORGE. Yeah, we'll just be moseyin' along now Miss *Switchblades*—I mean Miss Lady.

COYOTE SKIP. You have yourself a good night Miss Lady.

COYOTE BRUCE. Yeah. You have a good night Miss Lady.

COYOTE RAY. Deez woods be all yours now Miss *Death*—I mean—*Damn*—We just be movin' along now *Ma'am*.

COYOTE HAL. You give us a holler if you need anything Miss Lady.

COYOTE LARRY. Yeah. Give us a holler if you need anything Miss *Spaghetti Death*—I mean, Miss Le Mans lady.

COYOTE SCOTT. Hey guys, I think I saw some bunny rabbits that-a-ways.

COYOTE WAYNE. Yeah, more bunny rabbits that- a-ways guys. Let's go!

COYOTE STUPID. I din't see no bunny rabbits that-a-ways.

COYOTE CHRIS. *(harsh whisper)* Shut up, stupid!

COYOTE JEFF. Yes sirree, we'll be goin' now Miss Lady.

LADY. And so this gang of ky-otes who thought they were badass bitches found out the hard way they were just *bitches*, put their tails between their legs, and slowly slithered off into the night and as far away from my ten deadly switchblades as they could get.

THE DOPPEL-GANGERS

Over the next two weeks there was not ONE but TWO sightings of Lady that turned out to be doppelganger cats that looked so much like Lady even *I* was fooled. It was *weird*. It was *freaky*. It was *freaky ass weird*.

After the two doppelganger disappointments I became so despondent, gloomy, and depressed that the song *"It's the End of the World"* by Skeeter Davis began to loop over and over in my head and I couldn't stop it.

It's always darkest before
the dawn

The next day was the 33rd day of the search for Lady. I woke up, got coffee and breakfast at McDonald's, and then did absolutely *NOTHING*.

There was nothing left to do. I couldn't even think of anything else to do. I had done it all already. I had canvassed the entire neighborhood dozens of times day and night. I had hired a cat detective and did everything she said. I slept in the nature preserve all night long with the door ajar. I had encountered a freaky-ass night walker at 3AM. I taped "Lost Cat" postcards over the keyholes of every door in the neighborhood. But it was all pointless and in vain. Lady was gone, or *dead*, and I would never see her again.

I sat behind the wheel of *The Black Bat* and tried to process (in utter vain) how I could possibly go on without my *Best Friend*. Just then I received a random text from an "*Unknown Caller*." The text read:

We see your cat.
She's at 21870 San Fernando Ave.

The two doppelganger disappointments were still fresh in my mind so I didn't get too excited. I figured this was just another doppelganger cat and calmly called the number on my screen fully expecting this to be another false alarm. A middle-age Asian man answered the phone.

"Hello?"

"Hi, this is Z. Z. Le Mans, the owner of the cat."

"Oh, hi."

"Do you still see the cat?"

"Yes. She's sitting in the driveway of the address I sent you."

"Great. Listen. There have been some false sightings. Would you mind taking a snapshot of the cat with your cellphone and texting it to me?"

"Sure. No problem. I will do that now."

Three minutes later I received a text with a photo attachment. I casually opened the photo attachment expecting another doppelganger but—

It was Lady ! ! !

This time for sure. I recognized her custom collar. I quickly called the man back.

"Hello?"

"Yes! That's my cat! Do you still see her?"

"No. She disappeared behind the house."

"Okay. I'm on my way. Thank you!"

"Let us know if you find your cat. We have two cats of our own."

I raced to the address and got there in four minutes. I rang the doorbell of the house but no one was home. I didn't want to trespass into the back yard with no one home but under the circumstances did it anyway and called out to Lady over and over again.

No sight or sound of Lady.

I continued to call out to Lady and scoured the back yard for five minutes.

Still no sight or sound of Lady.

Shit. She's missing again! But she couldn't be far away and I could *feel* her presence. Lady was nearby somewhere. The backyard was a bust, so I walked up and down the street calling Lady's name for five minutes.

No sight or sound of Lady.

My heart sank and despair quickly returned. I just missed Lady by seconds and now I might be back at SQUARE ONE again. Defeated, I began walking back to my car. That's when I heard Lady's unmistakable "yap" and my heart filled with joy. Lady was close by but *where???* I couldn't see her.

I continued to walk toward the car and call out to Lady. Lady *yapped* again but this time the sound was *louder* and *closer*. But I still couldn't see Lady. I called out to Lady several more times and continued to walk toward the car. I was almost at the car when Lady *yapped* again and this time Lady sounded three feet away but I still couldn't see her! Then she *yapped* again, I turned to my right, and *WHAMMO!!!*

There was Lady!!!

Lady hobbled slowly toward me clearly worn out from her 33-Day ordeal.

"Well, it's about *time,*" she grumbled weakly. "I can't believe you *lost* me Mr. Man. I've been living under porches and tool sheds for a month. Your parenting skills suck donkey dicks."

"I'm sorry, Lady."

"Well, don't just stand there like an *idiot*; I'm tired, cold, and hungry; wrap me up in some warm blankets and bring me some *food.*"

HE LOOKS SUSPICIOUS

Lady and I were back together and living in *The Black Bat* daily which made us look *suspicious* to all the west Cupertino snobs who are overly suspicious by nature and desperately in need of a 30-Day stint in *"Suspicion Rehab"* to detox their minds of grossly unfounded suspicions, snob-filled arrogance, and chronic *xenophobia*.

911 OPERATOR. Emergency services. What are you reporting?

CALLER. There's a man. A *suspicious* man. In a suspicious black car. And he looks *suspicious*. And my *suspicions* tell me he is doing something *suspicious*.

911 OPERATOR. I see. Is he committing a *crime???*

CALLER. I just told you. He looks *suspicious*. That's a crime in Cupertino; I believe it's a felony; don't you know this *stuff???*

911 OPERATOR. Okay ma'am. Just sit tight. I'm sending a sheriff deputy to check this man out right now.

CALLER. Better send the SWAT team too.

911 OPERATOR. Does he have weapons???

CALLER. No, but he looks *suspicious*.

911 OPERATOR. Right, well, officers will be out there soon to check him out, ma'am.

CALLER. Wait, there's more.

911 OPERATOR. What else?

CALLER. He *stole* a cat.

911 OPERATOR. He *stole* a cat???

CALLER. Yes.

911 OPERATOR. How do you know he *stole* a cat?

CALLER. He has a cat in the car.

911 OPERATOR. Well, how do you know the cat was *stolen*?

CALLER. He looks *suspicious*. 10 to 1 the cat was *stolen*.

JUDITH WEST

The "caller" in the preceding chapter is a composite of all the west Cupertino snobs who want to run us out of town, especially *Judith West*, the *Queen Bee* of west Cupertino snobs.

The snobs of west Cupertino have taken the position that me, my cat, *The Black Bat*, our bohemian ways, and daily homeless struggle are an eyesore and blemish upon the affluent picturesque canvass of west Cupertino—and *worst* of all—*lower* property values!!!

What Judith West and the other west Cupertino snobs don't know is that my grandparents settled in west Cupertino in 1920 when west Cupertino was mostly fruit orchards, ranches, and farms.

Ed Traveras (a kid I grew up with) walks the R/R tracks at the corner of Stevens Creek Blvd. and Bubb Rd. in 1975. The same corner is completely unrecognizable today.

And when I grew up here in the 1970's Monta Vista was a humble blue-collar neighborhood where *everyone* knew *everyone* and *everyone* would give you the shirt off their back.

In those days nobody in Monta Vista judge anyone by their bank account, net worth, price tag of their home, the kind of car they drove, or what prestigious university their kid just got into. Only *snobs* think like that and there were NO snobs in Monta Vista and west Cupertino then.

That all changed in the 1980's and 1990's when the computer revolution turned Cupertino into a sea of high-tech industrial parks and affluent suburbs that became the "go to" for high-tech movers and shakers from all parts of the world. And if these high-tech movers and shakers weren't *snobs* when they got here *they soon would be* because by the 1990's west Cupertino had become the *Snob Capital* of the world!

Well, someone needs to tell Judith West and all the s*nobs* of west Cupertino to GO FUCK THEMSELVES and I got the job.

LADY. You tell 'em Mr. Man!

In an evil *underhanded* attempt to run me and my cat out of town Judith West began telling everyone I was a "*Drug Dealer*."

A Drug Dealer ? ! ? !

Judith West is a lying sack of shit the Devil shit out his ass and I will show her NO mercy. This sourpuss cuntface bitch has no idea I'm an award-winning writer but she's about to find out—the *HARD* way!

THE 3RD BASE CLUB

LIFE is a GAME (*similar to baseball*) and <u>THE 3RD BASE CLUB</u> is an elite private club for all the rich kids born on 3RD base.

Some of us didn't get that lucky in life. I wasn't even born in the *ballpark*. I was born across the street behind the liquor store next to the dumpster. My deadbeat alcoholic father once pointed a loaded gun at me drunk off his ass and that's a pretty good summary of my childhood.

I was born and raised in abject poverty by two dumbass dysfunctional parents, but that doesn't mean I'm *stupid*. I have an I.Q. in the top 5% percent of the world and have read over a thousand books. With affluent 3RD BASE parents I could have *been* anything, *done* anything. Instead, I'm living in my car with my cat.

What bothers me about the rich, spoiled, pampered, protected, arrogant, conceited, self-entitled members of the 3RD BASE CLUB is they all act like they hit a home run in *THE GAME of LIFE.*

They didn't.

They just got born on 3rd base.

Well, there's a BIG DIFFERENCE between:

A) Getting born on 3rd base

B) Hitting a HOME RUN over the center field
   fence

A) Requires *luck*—and well, let's face it; just *luck.*

B) Requires talent, courage, brains, resourcefulness, ingenuity, determination, perseverance, and *mettle*; tons and tons of *mettle.* More mettle than 3rd basers have.

And, as it turns out, A and B are intrinsically related to THE TWO PATHS of LIFE which I will delineate in the next chapter.

TWO LIFE
PATHS

THE TWO PATHS

The Golden Rule

"Do unto others as you would have them do unto you."

(found in *every* religion)

There are only two paths in LIFE — A and B

LIFE PATH A

The members of LIFE PATH A make MONEY their GOD and their LIFE GOALS are *Safety, Security,* and *Comfort.*

Due to childhood indoctrination most members of LIFE PATH A identify as their parent's religion, although few of them are religious and their identification with their family religion is a shallow proclamation with no real *belief* behind it.

The members of LIFE PATH A are not trying to make the world a better place—*that is the furthest thing from their mind.* The members of LIFE PATH A only care about making THEIR life better and don't give a flying fuck about *You, Me, Their Neighbors, or the World at Large.*

The members of LIFE PATH A see life as a ruthless *"Rat Race"* where *winning is everything,* and when two members of LIFE PATH A vie for the same piece of cheese it's gonna get ugly—*real* ugly—for the members of LIFE PATH A consider *The Golden Rule* a philosophy that exists only in the pages of religion and one that is not remotely practical or desirable in our greedy, cutthroat, dog-eat-dog world.

When viewed under a microscope the philosophy of LIFE PATH A is shockingly *Luciferian* and most members of LIFE PATH A are *Luciferians* whether they realize it or not!

Membership in LIFE PATH A requires the following character traits, skills, attitudes, and mindset:

- Greed

- Avarice

- Narcissism

- Herd Mentality

- The ability to jump through hoops like a trained seal

- *Fear-based* thinking whereby you make the *safest* decision at every crossroads and play THE GAME of LIFE as *safely* as it can possibly be played

- A *"Greedy Miser"* mindset whereby you take as much as you can and give as little as possible

- A thorough knowledge of POWER DYNAMICS whereby you kiss the ass of all those *above* you in power and shit on all those *below* you in power

- Your mental soundtrack blasts 24-7: Me, Me, Me, *Me, Me, Me, Me, Me, Me, Me, Me, Me, Me, Me, Me, Me, Me, Me, Me, Me, Me, Me, Me, Me, Me, Me.*

- Your idea of SUCCESS is graduating college, working 40+ hours a week at a job you hate, getting saddled with a 30 year mortgage, paying property taxes year after year, having 2.5 kids, sending your 2.5 kids to college, getting divorced, dividing assets in divorce court, getting remarried, getting divorced again, dividing assets in divorce court again, having a mid-life crisis, joining a gym in a futile attempt to stay young and attractive, getting old and selling your dream house to pay the astronomical monthly fee at the nursing home where you now live, slowly wasting away at the nursing home, feeling sad, lonely, feeble, and insignificant in your final days on this Earth, and wondering with your last dying breath if that's all there was to *Life,* or did *Life* have some *far* deeper meaning and purpose that somehow *escaped* you*???*

LIFE PATH B

In stark contrast to LIFE PATH A the members of LIFE PATH B make GOD their GOD and consciously choose careers and lifestyles that serve humanity and make the world a better place.

The members of LIFE PATH B view life as <u>*a daring adventure or nothing at all*</u> and enthusiastically embrace taking risks, innovation, thinking outside the box, and in many cases, *living* outside the box!

And since the members of LIFE PATH B are vastly more influential than members of LIFE PATH A, even a relatively small increase in LIFE PATH B membership would *dramatically* change the world for the better, and a *large* increase in LIFE PATH B membership would create *Heaven on Earth* virtually overnight!

Membership in LIFE PATH B requires the following character traits, skills, attitudes, and mindset:

- Belief in GOD or a Higher Power

- Love of Excellence

- Contempt for the *status quo, mediocrity, and* playing THE GAME of LIFE as *safely as possible*

- The *inability* to jump through hoops like a trained seal

- A burning desire to create, innovate, and make the world a better place

- The courage to break stupid laws and stupid rules in service of a Higher Truth and a Better World

- Your definition of SUCCESS is a job you love and making a difference in the world

- The realization that our world is rapidly becoming a dystopian nightmare and that our only hope is a radical *"New Renaissance"* before it's too late.

In 1973 a college hippie named Steve Jobs became disenchanted and disillusioned with LIFE PATH A, dropped out of college, adopted LIFE PATH B, and the rest is history . . .

THE GRADY TWINS

"Mr. Man?"

"Yeah?"

"I don't know about you, but I'm starting to get *Cabin Fever* living in the car for so long."

"Yeah. Me too, Lady."

"Remember when we watched *The Shining*?"

"Yeah."

"That guy went crazy from Cabin Fever."

"Yeah. I remember."

"He tried to kill his whole family with an axe."

"Yep. I know."

"You're not gonna go crazy from Cabin Fever and try 'n' kill me with an axe are you, Mr. Man???"

"No Lady, I'm not gonna kill you with an axe, but I could rip your arms and legs off with my manly manness."

"That's *not* funny, Mr. Man."

"Well, what about me, Lady??? What if <u>YOU</u> go crazy from Cabin Fever and slice 'n' dice me into chunky Mexican salsa with your 10 deadly switchblades???

"Good point, Mr. Man; I never thought of that. Wait a minute! Wait a minute! What if we *both* go crazy from Cabin Fever and murder each other in a murderfest of morbid magnitude???"

"Then we're *goners*, Lady.

"No, I'm *serious*, Mr. Man."

"Me too, Lady. If we *both* go mad from Cabin Fever and turn on each other in a murderfest of morbid magnitude it's gonna look like a slaughter house floor in here."

"Mr. Man, couldn't you just *lie* to me like all the other cat dads do and tell me everything is gonna be *fine* despite all evidence to the contrary?"

"Blowing smoke up your ass isn't my style, Lady. The ugly, cold, hard, truth served straight no chaser is my style."

"Yeah, I know, Mr. Man; it's just that I wish the ugly, cold, hard truth wasn't so *cold, hard,* and *ugly.*"

"Yeah, me too, Lady."

"Mr. Man?"

"Yeah?"

"If our Cabin Fever gets worse are the Grady twins gonna show up?"

"I hope not. It would be pretty crowded in here."

"For *reals,* Mr. Man."

"For *reals,* Lady. It would be pretty crowded in here."

"I hope the Grady twins don't show up. Those girls creep me out. Look, Mr. Man, as far as I'm concerned there's enough *creepiness* in the world. We don't need some *dead* girl ghosts showin' up and adding their brand of creepiness to an already creepy ass world. You catch my drift, Mr. Man?"

"I catch your drift, Lady."

"I mean, what kind of world is this, Mr. Man, where we have to worry about the Grady twins showin' up in their creepy ass baby blue dresses and creepin' the holy mother fuckin' shit out of us*???* I mean, our life's hard enough as it is, Mr. Man. Can't we just go about our homeless livin' in the car business without worrying about the Grady twins showin' up? We don't need no *dead* girls around here Mr. Man. We got enough *problems* as it is!"

"Good point, Lady."

"Mr. Man*?*"

"Yeah*?*"

"I just want you to know that if I *lose it* and turn you into a plate of spaghetti with my ten deadly switchblades the *Cabin Fever* made me do it."

"Thanks, Lady. That means a lot to me. Likewise, if I *lose it* and pull your arms and legs out of their sockets and mount your head on the dashboard for all to see, the *Cabin Fever* made me do it."

"Understood, Mr. Man. We love each other, but we might *kill* each other."

"That's the way it goes sometimes."

"Well, I guess that's it then."

"Yeah. I guess that's it then."

"Guess I'll go to bed now."

"Guess I'll go to bed now too."

95

"Goodnight, Mr. Man."

"Goodnight, Lady."

"See you in the mornin'."

"See you in the mornin'."

(long pause)

"Maybe."

DRINKING & DRIVING

"Mr. Man, do you really think you should be drinking and driving???"

"I'm not drinking and driving."

"You just had a big ass beer."

"That big ass beer was consumed in the parking garage in a parked position."

"And now you're driving."

"Exactly. I drank. And then I drove. I didn't drink and drive *simultaneously*."

"Yeah, I'm not a lawyer Mr. Man, but I think it amounts to the same thing."

"Lady, would you just concentrate on being a cat and stop being my mother."

"Sure, fine, whatever. Get us killed. See if I care."

"I'm not gonna get us killed. And besides, I have a rather loose interpretation of the law."

"So I've noticed."

"Man's Law means nothing to me."

"That's obvious."

"Cosmic Law is the only law that matters."

"God help us."

"Listen, drinking and driving gets a bad rap because losers and morons get shitface drunk and then drive. I don't get shitface drunk and I'm actually a better driver after a beer."

"A big ass beer."

"Fine. A big ass beer. I'm more relaxed. I go with the flow better. I use my horn less."

"Fine. Drink up Mr. Man. If you wanna get us killed in some hellacious accident of twisted metal, blood and bones, that's your business, but my death will be on your conscience and the karmic penalty will be severe."

"I'm not gonna get us killed."

"That's what they all say—right before the *impact*."

"Isn't it time for your nap Lady*???*"

"Fine. Get us killed. See if I care. Just make sure you spell my name right on my tombstone."

"It's pretty hard to misspell *Lady*."

"Not after a big ass beer."

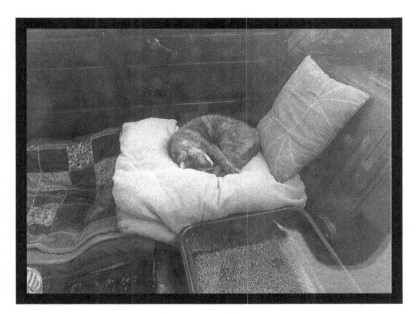

OUTSIDE THE BOX

Lady and I eventually got living in the car down to a science, but there were *two* problems I could never solve. Cat vomit and . . .

"*Lady!!!*"

LADY'S MIND. *Oh shit. He saw it. I'm toast.*

"Yeah, Mr. Man?"

"You peed outside the litterbox again *! ! !* "

"I *did?*"

"Don't give me that innocent crap. You *know* you did."

"My bad, Mr. Man."

"How can you pee outside the litterbox*???* The litterbox *is* huge!"

"Okay, well, I'm glad you brought that up Mr. Man 'cuz quite honestly, using that damn thing isn't as easy as it looks."

"*Huh???*"

"For one thing, it's not like my butt has eyes. I step into that damn thing, set my coordinates, get into position, make a few last minute adjustments, lock position, then fire away. But it's not an *exact* science. There's is a margin of *error* involved."

"A margin of *error???*"

"A 5% margin of error on a good day and a 10% margin of error on a bad day."

"Well, can you at least clean up your *errors* when you make them?"

"That would violate our *Terms of Agreement*, Mr. Man."

"What *Terms of Agreement???*"

"The *Terms of Agreement* we entered into when I first moved in."

"Refresh my memory."

"You do all the *hard* work and I do *NO* work."

THE HAUNTED HOUSE DREAM

A few days later I had the haunted house dream...

...the dream started with me walking barefoot on Stevens Creek Blvd. at 3AM toward the spooky old house I grew up in. My feet hurt from walking barefoot, but I endured the pain stoically and kept right on walking.

Why I was walking to my childhood home I had no idea, but something in the dream was pulling me there like a powerful magnet and I felt I had no choice but to go there.

When I arrived at the house the house looked far worse than when we lived there. In the dream the house had clearly been vacant for many years and all the exterior paint was badly chipped and half the windows were broken and boarded with sheets of weathered plywood. Our house was so old that our garage wasn't a garage at all but a "Carriage House" with a dirt floor.

I walked barefoot past the gateless gate and into our big dirtyard. I suddenly became very sleepy and tried to sleep on the dirt floor of the Carriage House. This was odd because I always felt that our Carriage House was haunted and never liked being in there alone.

However, I found it impossible to sleep in the Carriage House and soon walked to the back door of our house because we usually entered our house by the back door.

When I reached the back door I saw something a little spooky and unsettling—the door was unlocked and slightly *ajar*. Despite my apprehension I felt compelled to open the door and look inside. When I did I beheld a ghastly sight...

...empty liquor bottles, beer cans, litter, trash, and cigarette butts were strewn about everywhere. It was obvious that vagrants and party animals had been using our old home as a "crash pad" and "party pad" for many years. Despite this, vivid visions from my childhood and adolescence came to life before my eyes in holographic detail and the juxtaposition of scenes from NOW and THEN was eerie and unsettling and I just stood in the doorway and took it all in. It was a lot to take in.

I was about to enter when I heard a faint moan and the floorboards creaked down the hall. I froze. *Someone* was here. Or maybe it was my father's ghost. Either way, it was time to get the hell out of there and I began walking back to Stevens Creek Blvd. where the dream began, and as I walked barefoot along Stevens Creek Blvd. again I thought...

...Why did I come here??? What was I looking for??? What did I hope to find??? And did I find it???

I had no answers to any of those questions and the dream ended there.

BACK
ON FREUD'S
COUCH

The next day I was back on Freud's couch. I told Freud about the dream and asked, "What do you think it all *means???*"

Freud puffed on his cigar pensively and said, "Der are many zings to discuss here. Zet's start with zour vamily home. Da dream starts vith you valking to zour childhood home, vright?"

"Yeah."

"Zhat indicates a dezire to return to zour childhood. Do you zee zat?"

"I had a horrible childhood. Why would I want to go back?"

"Zou have some unfinished business there."

"Some unfinished business?"

"Jes. Zum unresolved issues. Ju have zum un- resolved issues in childhood. Dat's vie you returned to joor childhood home."

"What kind of unresolved issues?"

Freud puffed on his cigar and a plume of smoke bellowed out his mouth and danced in the smoke filled room. "Zou vent back to zat house to repair your childhood."

"Repair my childhood?"

"Jes."

"How would I do that?"

"Ju can't repair joor childhood. Zat's the problem. Ju went back to repair something zhat cannot be repaired. Za past is past. Zu can't change it."

"You're right. I can't change my childhood. It was what it was."

"Eggzacktly. But there's more..."

"More???"

"Jes."

"What?"

"Ju have a faddah complex."

"A father *complex???*"

"Jes."

"Can you explain a little about that."

"Ju rezent yor faddah."

"Yes."

"But ju also have a zeep fear that ju will become yor faddah."

That struck a chord.

"You're right. I've been afraid of becoming my father my entire life. What do I *do* about it?"

"Zhat's a complex anzwer and ver out of zime. Zet's leave zat for next veek's *zession* . . ."

A TRIP TO THE WEED DEALER

I'm not a weed guy. I'm a beer and wine guy. Nothing against weed. It's just not my thing. But living in the car with Lady was giving me migraine headaches. So, I decided to see if weed would reduce or eliminate those headaches. So, I drove back to Cupertino to visit my favorite liquor store because I knew the owner's son very well and knew that in addition to selling bottles of booze the son also sold weed *illegally* under the counter. For confidentiality I will call the son "Mike" and the shop *"Bottle & Bong Liquors."*

After a long drive all the way across town I parked *The Black Bat* at *"Bottle & Bong Liquors"* and walked through the automatic double glass doors. Mike was manning the counter as usual and playing *CALL of DUTY* on his gaming console.

ME. Hi Mike.

MIKE. Hey Z. Where you *been???*

ME. I moved to Milpitas.

MIKE. *Milpitas???* Why'd you move there???

I told Mike our sad story then said . . .

ME. I need some *weed.*

MIKE. *Weed???* You don't smoke weed.

ME. I know, but I'm getting migraine headaches living in the car with my cat. I'm hoping weed will cure my headaches.

MIKE. All I got right now is *Purple Haze;* you want some?

ME. *Purple Haze???* What's *that???*

MIKE. It's *purple* weed.

ME. *Purple* weed??? What happened to *green* weed???

MIKE. Green weed is still around, but all I have today is *purple* weed. You want some?

ME. When you gonna have *green* weed again?

MIKE. Maybe in two or three weeks.

ME. *Two or three weeks???*

MIKE. That's when I'll see the supplier again.

ME. I don't think I can wait that long. Yeah, hook me up with some *Purple Haze.*

MIKE. How much you want?

ME. Just gimme one joint for now. If it works I'll be back for more.

MIKE. You got it.

Just then a car pulled up in front of the store and two men got out. Mike looked at me and whispered,

MIKE. Go wait in your car. I'll roll you up and bring it out when I'm done with these guys.

ME. Thanks, man.

I went back to the car and waited with Lady.

LADY. What's goin' on, Mr. Man?

ME. I'm waitin' for some Purple Haze.

LADY. What's *Purple Daze???*

ME. Purple *Haze.*

LADY. I *said* that.

I explain Purple Haze to Lady.

Lady sighs heavily . . .

LADY. More *illegal* activity*???* Mr. Man can you *possibly* live within the confines of the *Law???* Who's gonna take care of me if you get busted and land your ass in *jail???*

ME. I'm not gonna get busted.

LADY. That's what Al Capone said.

ME. How do *you* know *Al Capone???*

LADY. We saw the Al Capone documentary on YouTube, *remember?*

ME. I forgot.

LADY. Be careful, Mr. Man. This Purple Daze deal could be an undercover set-up by the Feds. If you get busted by the Feds they're gonna fry your ass in the *electric chair* and then I'll be homeless and starve to death in a rainy dark dank alley next to some drunk homeless loser who vomits hot sticky whiskey gobbledy-goop all over my fur coat and then I'm gonna smell like hot whisky gobbledy-goop for the next three weeks and it'll be all your fault Mr. Man.

ME. Don't be so *melodramatic.*

LADY. I'm not being *monochromatic.*

ME. *Melodramatic.*

LADY. I *said* that; anyway, this crazy idea of yours seems pretty loony tunes if you ask me, Mr. Man.

ME. Whataya mean?

LADY. Well, as I understand it, Mr. Man, your plan is to fire-up this illegally acquired ratty ass dried up purple weed cigarette, take a big huge drag from this illegally acquired ratty ass dried up purple weed cigarette, then hold the smoke from this illegally acquired ratty ass dried up purple weed cigarette in your lungs for as long as you possibly can without dying or choking to death, then pray to the gods that by some funky ass miracle some funky ass "mystery shit" inside the funky ass smoke from the illegally acquired funky ass dried up purple weed cigarette interacts in some funky ass way with the funky ass wires and chemicals in your brain and then by some funky ass MAGIC no one really understands cures you of these funky ass margarine headaches. That's your plan, right???

ME. That is indeed my plan Lady, however, somehow the way you explain it, it sounds like a hare-brained idiotic idea from a psychedelic Bugs Bunny cartoon from a parallel reality.

LADY. That's because it sounds exactly like a hare-brained idiotic idea from a psychedelic Bugs Bunny cartoon from a parallel reality.

ME. Thanks, Lady.

LADY. As usual, Mr. Man, you are hell-bent on testing yet another one of your crazy misguided ideas and most likely getting us all killed in the process. I won't try to dissuade you from carrying out this crazy idea of yours Mr. Man since I know that would be pointless, but let me ask you one simple question: What if this hare-brained idiotic idea of yours doesn't work???

ME. Then it doesn't work.

LADY. That's *it???* No back-up *plan???*

ME. I've never had a back-up plan in my life.

LADY. Are these *margarine* headaches of yours really so bad that you need to resort to crazy ass cures like this?

ME. *Migraine* headaches.

LADY. I *said* that.

ME. Yes, they are.

LADY. How often do you get these *margarine* headaches?

ME. Three or four times per week.

LADY. *Three* or *four* times per week?!?! *Damn-a-Rama-Bama*, Mr. Man. Have you ever figured out what *causes* these *margarine* headaches of yours?

ME. Yeah.

LADY. What?

ME. *You.*

PURPLE
HAZE
AND THE
COSMIC
OCTOPUS

A few nights later I went to bed with a really bad migraine headache and it was time to put *Purple Haze* to the test. I pulled the *Purple Haze* joint out of the plastic bag and not familiar with *purple* weed smoked *half* the joint in two minutes.

Big Mistake

In two minutes I didn't know my name. Two minutes later I didn't even know what planet I was on. And two minutes after that I *astral projected* into outer space where I found myself floating in a colorful sea of stars, galaxies, and nebulae.

I no longer felt myself. More accurately, I no longer felt my *Self*. I no longer had a *Self* to feel. There was no more *Me* there. There was no more *Me* there at all. It was as if I had become *pure consciousness* and stripped of all *personality*.

I suddenly realized I was having a classic *"Ego Death"* experience that I had read about so many times in my esoteric studies. Try as I might, I could not say or think the thought *I* or *Me*. There was no *I* or *Me* there. The *feeling* was unsettling and liberating at the same time. Then I heard *The Professor's* voice say to me *telepathically* . . .

> *"You are a part of the ALL and the EVERYTHING.*
> *You always have been. And you always will be."*

Then a massive shape appeared before me that loosely resembled a giant octopus. The head of the octopus glowed bright white and the eight tentacles were descending degrees of *gray* and *black* at the tips. *The Professor* continued,

> "What you see before you is a simplistic model of the *Omniverse* that your finite mind can understand. *God and*

the Omniverse are One and the Same thing. There is *no* difference. There is *no* separation between *God, Matter, Time, and Space.* It is all *One.* Every atom in the Universe in a part of *God* and *God* is present in every atom of the Universe. The head of the octopus, as you call it, glows bright white because it is the godhead and pure *God.* The tentacles represent Man's *ego.* The further away Man is from God the *stronger* and *darker* is his ego. The closer Man is to God the *less* ego he has to darken his *Soul* and his *Soul* naturally resides closer to the Godhead. The purpose of *reincarnation* is self-improvement lifetime after lifetime and thus Man has the opportunity to move *closer* and *closer* to the Godhead with each passing life if he lives his life *wisely.* The ultimate goal of *reincarnation* is to unite with the Godhead and become *One* with *God.* This state of perfection is called *Moksha* and when Man achieves *Moksha* he reincarnates no more forever. Thus, life is merely a *GAME* of reunification with God and with every incarnation Man will either be moving *toward* or *away* from the ultimate goal of life. Do you have any *questions?*"

"*N-No,*" I stammered, awed by the magnitude of the lesson.

"Very well," The Professor quipped. Then he telepathically directed my attention toward a thick cluster of twinkling stars, galaxies, and nebulae and said, "Remember this *equation* always. Just then a group of bright shimmering stars began to spin and twirl in the heavens and arranged themselves into a startling mathematical equation.

The equation was ...

God = Man - Ego

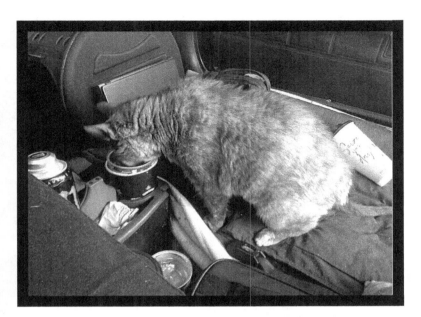

THE GRASS IS GREENER

Many people think the grass is greener over there and Lady has a chronic case of this psychological malady . . .

Lady and I are having brunch. Lady has her cat food and I have a bag of "goodies" from the grocery store.

I remove goodie #1 from the bag. Lady stops eating her cat food and says, "What's that Mr. Man?"

"It's a three cheese bagel."

"Lemme see that..."

Lady sniffs the three cheese bagel and takes a bite. "Mmmmm. Tasty! I like cheese."

Lady takes two more bites of my three cheese bagel then goes back to her cat food. A few moments later I pull out goodie #2 from my bag. Lady stops eating her cat food and says,

"What's *that* Mr. Man?"

"It's a mozzarella stick."

"What's a *monster-ella* stick???"

"*Mozzarella* stick."

"I *said* that."

"It's a stick of *cheese.*"

"You know I like *cheese*; gimme some of dat."

"Here."

Lady takes several bites of my mozzarella stick then goes back to her cat food. A few moments later I pull out goodie #3 from my bag. Lady stops eating her cat food and says,

"What's *that* Mr. Man?"

"It's a nectarine."

"What's a *never-being???*"

"*Nectarine.*"

"I *said* that."

"It's a type of fruit."

"Lemme see that *thing.*"

Lady takes a bite of my nectarine and spits it out.

"I don't like *never-beings.*"

A few moments later I pull out goodie #4 from my bag. Lady stops eating her cat food and says, "What's that Mr. Man?"

"Potato chips. You don't like potato chips."

"How do you *know???*"

"I gave you potato chips when we first met. You didn't like them."

"I don't remember that."

"Here."

Lady takes a bite of potato chip and spits it out.

"I don't like potato chips."

"I told you."

"I forgot."

A few moments later I pull out goodie #5 from my bag. Lady stops eating her cat food and says, "What's that Mr. Man?"

"Red licorice."

"Red *liquor...lacor...lipor...*what is it*???*"

"*Here.* Just try some."

Lady looks it over cautiously.

"It looks like red *plastic.*"

"*Try* it *!*"

Lady takes a bite and spits it out.

"It *tastes* like red plastic*!*"

Lady goes back to her cat food and a few moments later I pull out the LAST goodie in my bag. Lady stops eating her cat food and says, "What's that Mr. Man*?*"

"A glazed donut."

"What's a *dazed* donut*?*"

"*Glazed* donut."

"I *said* that."

"It's very *sweet;* you wouldn't like it."

"I'll decide what I *like* and what I *don't* like, Mr. Man. Gimme some of dat."

"*Here.*"

Lady takes a bite of the glazed donut, her face lights up like a Christmas tree, her mouth opens wide like the shark from JAWS, her eyes roll back in her head, and her teeth tear the donut to shreds.

Never underestimate the power of a glazed donut!

THE EVEREST
DREAM

The night of November 5, 2019 I went to bed as usual and had the Everest dream . . .

. . . the dream began with me and 20 other climbers at the base of Mount Everest. We came from all parts of the world and paid a lot of money to climb Mount Everest on a commercial expedition complete with all the guides, sherpas, cooks, food, equipment, oxygen tanks, boots, sleeping bags, tents, tools, ropes, pitons, etc. we would need to conquer Mount Everest. Day #3 of the climb I was surprise to find myself in the #2 position just behind our lead guide Dennis who had more Everest conquests than any of the other guides on our expedition. Dennis looked about 37 or 38 years old and reminded me of *"Bodhi"* the philosophical surfer dude played by Patrick Swayze in the 1991 movie *"POINT BREAK."* Dennis and I connected immediately. We were two philosophical bohemian Buddhists who didn't give a rat's ass about money, material things, feeling accepted by others, and all the other meaningless crap that most people want and need to feel secure in this world. We both lived outside the normal paradigms of *Society* and loved it. About halfway up Everest I began to see frozen dead climbers along the trail and it unnerved me a little.

"Dennis. These guys are *dead."*

"I know."

"When did this all happen*???"*

Dennis then pointed at each dead climber,"That guy's been here 3 years. That guy's been here 5 years. That guy's been here 8 years. And that guy's been here 12 years."

"Why don't they remove the bodies*???"*

"It's too difficult and too dangerous. The only way to remove the bodies is by helicopter and most pilots fear the crags, wind, and sudden snow storms of Everest could cause a crash. And for what*???* A dead body*???* No. Very few pilots are willing to risk their lives for a dead body."

"So they just stay here...*forever ? ? ?* "

"Yep."

"That's kinda gross."

"I depends on how you look at it, Z. These men were all *serious* climbers. Most would prefer to remain on Everest for all eternity than be buried in the ground back home."

"It's just fucking gross to see *dead* climbers on our ascent Dennis. Is this supposed to make me feel *good???*"

Dennis narrowed his gaze and sized me up a moment.

"Z, why did you come here?"

"To conquer Everest."

Dennis laughed uproariously.

"No one's ever conquered Everest. Just ask this guy," and Dennis kicked the dead climber in front of us *hard*.

"Then *why* did I come here???"

"You came here for the *secret* reason everyone comes here."

"And what's *that???*"

"To conquer *yourself*. And if you concur yourself Everest rewards you with the summit."

"And if I *don't* concur myself???"

"Then you become *this* guy," and Dennis kicked the dead climber hard again."

A crackling intensity filled the air.

"Now that you know *why* you came to Everest, are you ready to continue???"

I nodded my head slowly.

The next three days of climbing were agonizingly difficult and several in our group gave up and headed back with the help of two of our guides, but I remembered what Dennis had taught me, and what I was here for, and so I kept going. I continued to hold second position behind Dennis. I found comfort staring at his boots and emulating his exact steps. I felt as if I was following a great guru who had much to teach me.

Suddenly Dennis stopped to catch his breath and take in the view of the snow-capped Himilayan crags which were breathtakingly glorious and filled one with the awe, wonder, and majesty of *Nature*. The views on Everest made me want to do something *great* with my life n not squander it on meaningless things as so many people do.

"If we're lucky we'll reach The Lodge tonight," Dennis said in a breath of white fog.

"The *Lodge???*" I said quizzically.

"The Lodge marks the halfway point of the climb. It was built by sherpas in the mid-60s."

"It's a lodge with rooms, beds, heating, and running water?"

Dennis laughed. "No. Nothing like that. It's a shell of a building. No doors. No windows. No beds. No heating. But it's a roof over our heads for the night and the only roof we're gonna have over our heads for the entire trip so enjoy it. The Lodge also does a pretty good job blocking the wind. The Lodge is a welcome sight to veteran climbers."

Interesting, I thought. I couldn't wait to see this 'Lodge' but dusk was setting in fast and Dennis was worried that we might have to set camp before reaching The Lodge. But the gods were on our side. We soon saw something that looked like a house on the horizon. "That's The Lodge!" Dennis announced. We made it!" I got so excited I passed Dennis up and headed straight for *The Lodge* determined to be the first one in our group to enter *The Lodge.*

The Lodge greeted me with a doorless doorway and bare wood. I passed the threshold of the door and beheld a large empty room of bare wood. I then noticed a second doorless doorway in the far left corner and walked toward it to see what was in there. I stepped through the second doorway and beheld a room similar to the first room but with one major change. This second room contained nine life-like statues of climbers! Wow. How odd, I thought. Who would go through all the trouble of lugging these heavy statues up to the lodge and what could be the purpose of these statues??? It seemed ludicrous that the statues were here at all. As I got closer to the statues I marveled more and more at their life-like detail. The sculptor that created these statues was clearly a sculptor of the highest order. I could hardly tell the difference between these lifeless statues and real living climbers. And then it hit me. These weren't statues. These were frozen climbers!!! I got sick to my stomach and rushed off to tell Dennis the bad news.

"Dennis! There's a problem."

"What???"

"There are frozen climbers in the lodge."

"I know."

"You *know* ! ! ! "

"They've been there for years."

"And they just stay there???"

"What do you want to do with them???"

I didn't have an answer.

"Z. It's the same as the dead bodies along the trail. It's better to leave them there. That's the way they would want it. The Lodge is a shrine to all the climbers who didn't make it."

This was all too weird and I thought I might be dreaming.

Half the group slept in room #1 and half the group slept in room #2 with the dead climbers. Of course, Dennis and I slept in room #2 with the dead climbers. As Dennis and I settled into our sleeping bags, my head was literally four inches away from a dead climber's boot.

"This is *creepy*, Dennis."

"Maybe, but think of it this way Z, they remind us what we're up against."

We all rose at dawn the next morning and at breakfast Dennis said if all went well we would reach the summit around 2PM. That got me very excited. Up to this point reaching the summit of Everest seemed like some foggy vague idea, wishful thinking, a pipe dream, a fantasy, but now it was just a few hours away. After breakfast there was electricity in the air and everyone was smiling and in good spirits.Dennis shouted, "Everyone! Listen up! We depart for the summit in ten minutes!" It was as if he had said, "We depart for *God* in ten minutes." After Dennis' announcement we all looked at each other with a mixture of excitement and dread. Everyone knew that the final leg to the summit was the most difficult—and the most *deadly*.

Ten minutes later Dennis called a huddle. "Listen up! You all know the final leg to the summit is the most *deadly* and we don't want any deaths on this expedition. 2PM is the deadline to reach the summit. If you haven't reached the summit by 2PM you must stop and turn back. It is *suicide* to try to reach the summit after 2PM. Do you understand?

"Yes," we replied rather weakly and sloppily.

"*DO YOU UNDERSTAND* ! ! !" Dennis roared.

"*YES* ! ! !" we replied tight unison.

"Then let's head out," he said, "And may the *gods* be with us."

And so at 7:30AM our expedition began the final ascent toward the summit of Mount Everest. The entire group was making good time up the perilous long last ridge toward the summit when Dennis and I got into a groove and pulled away from the pack reaching the summit first at 1:09PM.

The view from the top of Everest was spectacular beyond words and Dennis and I exchanged a teary-eyed "Bro-Hug" of triumph.

It's hard to describe the feeling I had there, in that moment, on summit top of Everest; it was a cocktail of so many thoughts and emotions. I had concurred myself, and as a reward for concurring myself Everest gave me the gift of the summit just as Dennis said it would.

Then Dennis asked me a very strange question, "Z. You're on the top of the world. What do you *see???*"

What do I see??? What did he mean, 'What do I *see???*' Bewildered, I turned very slowly 360 degrees and took it all *in*...

... the deep blue sky, the snow-capped crags, the white birds soaring effortlessly in the valley below. It was all so beautiful. Then it hit me. And I knew the answer to his question. *None of it was real.* It was all a *dream*. No, not *this* kind of dream. Not the dream of *sleep*. What I saw crystal clear on top of Mount Everest was the dream of *Maya*, the *Cosmic Dream* spoken of in The Tripitaka, The Upanishads, The Tibetan Book of the Dead, Kalachakra, The Heart Sutra, Rig Veda, The Bhagavad Gita, The Mahabharata, The Tao Te Ching, the poems of Ralph Waldo Emerson, The Urantia Book, Autobiography of a Yogi, the talks of Alan Watts, A Course in Miracles (*and others*) had taught me the ZENITH of all TRUTH:

Life is a dream and we are the imagination of ourselves.

And so there on the summit of Mount Everest I answered Dennis' strange question with an equally strange answer:

"I see my *Self,*" I said.

Dennis smiled. "Very good, Z. You passed the *Test.* You can go *back* now..."

Go *back* now*???* What did he mean *go back now???*

Suddenly Dennis' face and clothing morphed into the face and clothing of *The Professor* and with shock and amazement I realized that Dennis had been *The Professor* in disguise all along.

A PARKING GARAGE CHRISTMAS

December 24, 2019

LADY. What's our plans for Christmas, Mr. Man?

ME. We're gonna chill here in the parking garage.

LADY. Ha-ha. Funny. No, seriously, what are our plans this Christmas?

ME. I told you. We're gonna chill here in the parking garage.

LADY. I thought you were *joking.*

ME. Nope.

LADY. So, we're just gonna *chill* here in the parking garage*???* What kind of Christmas is *that???*

ME. I believe it's called *"The Parking Garage Christmas."*

LADY. Yeah, well, the parking garage Christmas sucks donkey dicks*!!!*

MR. MAN. I know.

Lady sighs.

LADY. Our life sucks donkey dicks, Mr. Man.

ME. I know.

LADY. When is our life gonna stop suckin' donkey dicks*???*

ME. When the gods decide to bless us with their bounty.

LADY. Well tell the goddamn gods to hurry up; our bounty's overdue*!*

ME. I did.

LADY. What'd they say?

ME. I haven't heard back from them.

LADY. Mr. Man, why is all this bad shit happening to us? We never hurt anyone.

ME. It's our *dharma*, Lady.

LADY. *Huh???*

ME. It's our *dharma.*

LADY. What's *dogma?*

ME. *Dharma!*

LADY. I *said* that.

ME. In Buddhism *dharma* refers to the unique challenges, trials, and tests the gods send you to develop your soul and character in this life.

LADY. Our *dogma* sucks donkey dicks!

ME. Yeah. I know.

> *Lady glances over at her empty food bowl.*

LADY. I'm hungry. What's for dinner?

ME. I got you something *special* for Christmas.

LADY. *Special???*

ME. Yeah.

LADY. I like the *sound* of *that.* Wud-ya get me*???*

ME. I got you a can of *"Friskies Seafood Platter."*

LADY. A can of *"Friskies Seafood Platter???"*

ME. Yeah.

LADY. Mr. Man, you know I prefer *"Friskies Poultry Platter."*

ME. I know, but the supermarket was out of *"Friskies Poultry Platter."*

LADY. Whadaya mean the supermarket was out of *"Friskies Poultry Platter???"*

ME. They were out.

LADY. The supermarket is *huge!* How could they be out of *anything???*

ME. Well Lady, apparently there was a rush on *"Friskies Poultry Platter"* for the holidays and a sea of crazed shoppers bought up all the cans of *"Friskies Poultry Platter."*

LADY. You mean a bevy of bitches bought all the cans of *"Friskies Poultry Platter?!?!"*

ME. Well, in all fairness, they might not be *bitches.*

LADY. Whaddaya mean they might not be *bitches???* They bought all the cans of *"Friskies Poultry Platter"* and didn't leave me *one* can for Christmas. They're *mega bitches!!!*

ME. Calm down, Lady, calm down. *"Friskies Seafood Platter"* isn't so bad. I know you like *"Friskies Seafood Platter."*

LADY. Yeah, I like *"Friskies Seafood Platter,"* but not as much as I like *"Friskies Poultry Platter."*

ME. I know, but it's an *imperfect* world, Lady; we don't always get what we want. Let's just be grateful for what we *have* this Christmas.

LADY. For what we *have???* Look around you Mr. Man; we have *nothing!!!*

ME. That's not true Lady; we have each other.

LADY. Mr. Man, all this Buddhism has made you content with *nothing*—and so we have *nothing*.

ME. All Buddha had was a *cave*.

LADY. Yeah, and Buddha froze his *ass* off in that cave!

ME. Lady, there are some things more important in life than worldly possessions and material comforts.

LADY. Like *what???*

ME. Truth. Beauty. The eternal verities.

LADY. Verities *schmerities*, Mr. Man. All I want out of life is a can of *"Friskies Poultry Platter"* and a live moose to play with.

ME. *Mouse.*

LADY. I *said* that.

ME. I got you that toy mouse.

LADY. That beat-up old thing? I don't like it. It's *fake*. I want a *real* moose. One I can bat around for 40-minutes and then bite its head off.

ME. Lady, we've talked about this a *million* times. Murdering mice is bad karma.

LADY. Karma *shmarma*, Mr. Man. I'm a lady tiger. I need to express my mojo and primal energies from time to time.

ME. I'm worried about you, Lady. In your life review the Lords of Karma are gonna say, "Miss Lady. Why did you brutally murder and dismember 1 black bear, 27 coyotes, 19 lizards, 12 birds, and 36 mice in the life just lived?"

LADY. And I'm gonna look those old buzzards in the eye and say, "Because it was *fun* man!!!"

OH SHIT

I knew this was gonna happen one night and it did. Middle of the night. 3AM. I gotta poop and there's no place to poop. All public restrooms are closed. What-a-ya do? I knew this would happen eventually but I had no plan for that eventuality. So here I was. I needed to poop. And I really couldn't hold it any more. I really only saw two options. Dump my cargo outside in the bushes and risk being arrested for indecent exposure and performing a lewd act in public OR poop in Lady's litter box.

What this really came down to was . . .

Thoroughly embarrassing, humiliating, degrading, disgusting
<u>OPTION #1</u>

OR

Thoroughly embarrassing, humiliating, degrading, disgusting
<u>OPTION #2</u>

After weighing the *Pros* and *Cons* of both options I decided to poop in Lady's litter box and began to jostle and position myself over Lady's litter box at 3:02AM doing my best NOT to wake up Lady. Unfortunately, try as I might, sufficient noise was made during this process that Lady began to stir from a sound sleep and slowly became aware that something very odd, very weird, and very abnormal was going down in the car. Lady opened her eyes, yawned wide, and mumbled,

"What's goin' on, Mr. Man?"

"Nothing. Just go back to sleep."

"Why are you straddled over my litter box like that?"

"It's a new stretch I learned on YouTube yesterday. It's called 'The Squat Stretch.' I'm tryin' it out."

"It looks more like 'The Squat 'n' Leave It.' You're not gonna take a dump in my litterbox are you Mr. Man?"

"No. Now go back to sleep Lady."

"That's my litter box Mr. Man. That's *my* private litterbox for *my* private personal business. It is *not* an 'All-Species' litterbox."

"I'm aware of that Lady. I'm not gonna poop in your litter box. Now would you go back to sleep and mind your own business."

"How can I mind my own business when you're about to do some *business* in my *business* box."

Meanwhile, things were getting urgent down there and Lady kept babbling on like a woman on the phone. "Listen, Mr.

Man. There's a Comic Law about mixing *businesses*. If your *business* mixes with my *business*, and my *business* mixes with your *business*, and our *businesses* mix together in unholy *business* mixing yucky *yuckiness* for more than three seconds, the Earth will be destroyed by a big fiery fireball from the Heavens that will turn every living thing into crispy critter charcoal crispy critterness. It's in *The Bible*."

"That's an Old Testament prophesy Lady and probably not true. At any rate, we're gonna hafta risk it 'cuz I gotta poop and I gotta poop bad."

"This is so wrong Mr. Man. Reconsider before it's too *late ! ! !*"

"It's too late Lady. I've already set my coordinates. You know how that goes. The pooping process has begun. There's no turning back . . ."

"For the love of God, Mr. Man *turn back ! ! !*"

"Would you stop watching and give me some *privacy ! ! !*"

But Lady didn't stop watching. Instead, she looked on fascinated at what I was attempting to do and seemed deeply curious to see if I could actually pull it off without making a mess of things. That was it. I couldn't hold my heavy load of cargo any more and so I dropped my load of cargo into Lady's litterbox where it landed with a heavy *thud*.

"That's *gross* Mr. Man."

"Sorry Lady. There was no other choice."

"You could have gone behind the bushes."

"Right. My bad."

Then Lady screamed, "Oh god!!!"

"What???"

"Your poop stinks!!!"

"Sorry."

"Did you cover???"

"Not yet."

"Cover that shit!!!"

I then covered my poop with kitty litter using a paper coffee cup. I still needed to wipe my butt, but when I went to wipe my butt I realized to my shock and horror that I had *nothing* to wipe my butt with.

Shit.

No subject is terrible if the story is true,
if the prose is clean and honest, and if it
affirms courage and grace under pressure.

Ernest Hemingway

CHEESEBURGERS, JAILBAIT, AND A MOTEL

As our homeless saga continued I got hungry and pulled into a local IN-N-OUT BURGER and drove out with two cheeseburgers and a chocolate shake. It was a very hot day so I parked in the shade of some palm trees at an adjacent motel to eat my lunch.

Mid-burger I noticed a sandy blonde teenage girl walking toward us. She was maybe 16 or 17 and had the look and aura of a street smart girl who had been around the block a few times (*if you know what I mean*). She was a strikingly good-looking girl and as she drew near we exchanged smiles and then she said . . .

GIRL. Cool car.

ME. Thanks.

GIRL. Oh! You have a cat! She's cute.

LADY. That's right. I'm cute. Now get lost. He's *mine!*

GIRL. What's her name?

ME. Lady. What's your name?

GIRL. Rachel.

ME. I'm Z.

RACHEL. Why do you have your cat with you*???*

ME. I take my cat wherever I go.

RACHEL. What are you doing here?

ME. Just got some lunch at IN-N-OUT BURGER. What are *you* doing here?

RACHEL. I'm staying at this motel with my parents. We're on our way to L.A. for my cousin's wedding.

ME. Where are your parents?

LADY. Careful Mr. Man. She's underage.

ME. We're just talking. Stop being my *mother.*

RACHEL. They went shopping at The Great Mall. It's some famous mall in town.

ME. Yeah. I've been there. Why didn't you go shopping with them?

RACHEL. With my parents*???* Are you kidding*???* I'd rather poke my eye out with a rusty fork.

LADY. Forget it, Mr. Man, she's saving herself for marriage.

I almost burst out laughing.

Rachel and I enjoyed 20 minutes of witty banter that got a little spicy toward the end. At that point she became restless, fidgety, and looked me up and down on the sly.

RACHEL. Do you have a lighter?

ME. Yeah.

RACHEL. I got some weed in the room. You wanna blaze up?

MY LIBIDO. *Fuck yeah ! ! !*

ME. That sounds like fun, but I'm gonna hafta pass. Thanks anyway.

RACHEL. Alright, well, too bad. I guess I'll be *going* then. It was nice meeting you.

ME. It was nice meeting you too.

As Rachel walked away she waved goodbye to Lady.

RACHEL. Bye Lady!

LADY. Bye *bitch*.

Then Rachel swagged up the motel stairs and out of my life forever . . .

LADY. I'm proud of you, Mr. Man. You showed good character there.

ME. Thanks, Mom.

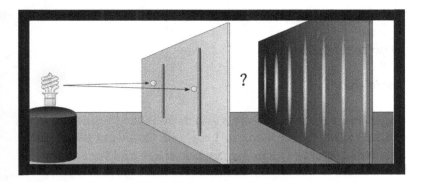

THE MAGIC OF QUANTUM MECHANICS

A BIG part of *"Self-Improvement"* is learning NEW things. So, I have spent my entire life learning NEW things. Even living in the car I wanted to learn NEW things. So around this time in our homeless odyssey I watched a dozen videos on *Quantum Mechanics* at the Milpitas Library.

That was a Game Changer

I saw many things in Quantum Mechanics that would help us get out of this homeless nightmare and shared this newfound hope with Lady . . .

"Quantum Mechanics is gonna solve all our problems, Lady."

"What's Quantum *Mechiccups???*"

"Quantum *Mechanics.*"

"I *said* that."

"Quantum Mechanics models and defines the building blocks of *Reality.* Moreover, near as I can tell, Quantum Mechanics holds the secrets of alchemy, teleportation, and time travel."

"We don't need *time travel*, Mr. Man; we need a *home.*"

"Quantum Mechanics is gonna get us a home."

"How is Quantum *Mechiccups* gonna get us a home???"

"I see a way to use *Probability Waves* to our advantage."

"What are Probability *Babes???*"

"Probability *Babes* are girls on Tinder. That's *not* what I said. I said Probability *Waves.*"

"I said *waves.*"

"No, you said *babes.*"

"I said *waves.*"

"You said *babes!*"

"I said *waves!*"

"You said *babes!*"

"*Waves!*"

"*Babes!*"

"*Waves!*"

"*Babes!*"

"*Waves!*"

"*Babes!*"

Ugh ! ! !

Cat for Sale...Cheap ! ! !

"So, what are *they???*"

"What are *what???*"

"Probability *Babes.*"

Ugh ! ! ! ! ! ! ! ! ! ! ! ! !

"Probability Waves are all the potential *realities* of a grouping of atomic particles at a given point in *Time* and *Space.*"

"Huh?"

"You see Lady, according to Quantum Mechanics, all potential outcomes of a Probability Wave exist *simultaneously* until the Probability Wave collapses on ONE of those probabilities and then *Reality* itself becomes the holographic representation of *that* probability. Are you with me so far?"

"You lost me at Probability *Babes*."

"Hold on Lady. It gets even better. Guess what collapses Probability Waves?"

"*Earthquakes?*"

"Your *thoughts.*"

"I don't have any *thoughts.*"

"I know but some people *do* and their *thoughts* collapse *Probability Waves!*"

Lady sighs in frustration.

"I don't see how any of this *helps* us, Mr. Man."

"Listen, Lady, the discovery of *Quantum Mechanics* was groundbreaking because it meant that our thoughts affect *Reality.*"

"Who *cares;* I'm hungry. When do we *eat?*"

"Think about it, Lady. If a man can alter *reality* with his thoughts then he can train his mind to manipulate reality like *putty!* He can teleport anywhere in the Universe by *thought* alone! He can *materialize* or *dematerialize* any object at will. He could even pass an elephant through the eye of a needle and the elephant would be no worse for wear!"

"*Ummm. Mr. Man???*"

"Yeah?"

"You haven't been smoking more of that *Pimple Haze* have you???"

"Never mind, Lady. *Metaphysics* is light-years beyond your comprehension."

"*Metafishsticks???* I thought this was *Quantum Mechicc-ups?* Get your terminology straight, Mr. Man. Is this mumbo jumbo *Quantum Mechiccups* or *Metafishticks???*

"It's *both* Lady. It turns out *Quantum Mechanics* IS *Meta-physics.*"

"Whoa."

"Major *whoa.*"

7 Mind-Blowing FACTS about

QUANTUM MECHANICS

MIND BLOWING FACT #1

Everything we know about Quantum Mechanics was discovered in the 1920's. There has been very little progress in Quantum Mechanics since then. This proves something I have been saying for years. People in the 1920's were way smarter than people today.

MIND BLOWING FACT #2

Quantum particles can be a *particle* or a *wave* and easily switch back and forth at will. *Huh??? What???* Isn't that *impossible???* According to your 3rd grade science book that is indeed *impossible*, but in the mysterious psychedelic world of *Quantum Mechanics* it happens all the time. Adding to the mystery is the fact that history's greatest quantum physicists have no idea *why* or *how* this happens and are as mystified as you are. *Hmmm.* Sounds like MAGIC to me.

MIND BLOWING FACT #3

Quantum particles can be in an infinite number of places at the *same* time. *Huh???* You heard right. *A quantum particle can be in an infinite number of places at the same time* and the world's greatest physicists have no idea *Why* or *How* that is possible. *Hmmm.* Sounds like MAGIC to me.

MIND BLOWING FACT #4

Inside the atom *electrons* instantaneously *teleport* from orbit to orbit and no physicist knows *Why* or *How* electrons do this. But since the teleportation is *instantaneous* and transcendental to *Time* physicists theorize that the electron must either be moving *faster* than the speed of light OR transcending *Time* entirely by some means unknown to modern science. *Hmmm.* Sounds like MAGIC to me.

MIND BLOWING FACT #5

Inside the subatomic world of the atom *electrons* often *disappear* and then *reappear* seconds later. Quantum Physicists say that's *weird.* In fact, they say that's *really* weird*!* And 100 years later the world's leading Quantum Physicists are still scratching their heads about what the fuck is going on with these *disappearing* electrons*!!!* And since Quantum Physicists don't like unanswered questions they have come up with a "theory" about the *disappearing* electrons that's right out of a Science Fiction novel. Their latest and greatest *theory* is that the *disappearing* electrons *teleport* to other worlds when they're gone*!!!* In Quantum Physics this is called *"The Many Worlds Theory."* I would have called it the *"Holy Fuckin' Shit Magic is REAL Theory"* but nobody asked me.

MIND BLOWING FACT #6

Part of Quantum Physics is called *"quantum entanglement."* This happens when quantum particle (A) gets entangled with quantum particle (B) and then the two particles become entangled and then *effect* and *countereffect* each other for all *eternity* even if you place them 500,000 light-years apart. The great Albert Einstein hated *"Quantum Entanglement"* because he couldn't explain WHY it happened and famously called it *"Spooky Action at a Distance."* But isn't that just another way of saying *MAGIC ? ? ?*

MIND BLOWING FACT #7

Quantum particles move in patterns called *"Probability Waves"* and these probability waves are essentially *Liquid Reality.* While in wave form the probability wave represents all possible outcomes until the wave form collapses on itself and becomes physical reality. So, *how* do probability waves decide what the *final* outcome will be*???* They *don't.* YOU do. YOU collapse the Probability Wave with your *thoughts.* This was 100% proven in *"The Double-Slit Experiments"* of the 1920's.

At the end of the day *Quantum Mechanics* proved something mystics, metaphysicians, and gurus have been saying for *thousands* of years . . .

Your THOUGHTS
Create Your REALITY

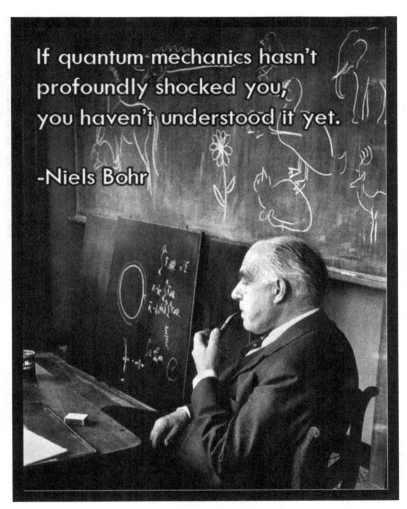

If quantum mechanics hasn't profoundly shocked you, you haven't understood it yet.

-Niels Bohr

Niels Bohr, Nobel Prize Physics, 1922

THE DUMPSTER
DEMON

During our homeless years Lady and I lived in *four* cities: Cupertino, Santa Clara, Milpitas, and Los Altos. This chapter explains *why* we left Milpitas for *good*.

Lady and I lived in the big 4-story Milpitas Library parking garage for 1½ years and that parking garage was a popular haven for dozens of homeless people living in their cars just like us. However, our tenure at the Milpitas Library parking garage came to an abrupt END on:

February 12, 2020 @ 11:31pm

At precisely that time a squad of eight Milpitas police cars entered the parking garage and the Milpitas police *evicted* *everyone* living in their cars including Lady and I.

Thus at 11:44PM, and without warning, Lady and I had to find a place to crash on this freezing cold night. I had to think quickly and suddenly remembered a creepy old abandoned strip mall several blocks away. I figured that would do for *tonight* and then we would relocate back to Cupertino in the morning.

I wasn't sure how *legal* it was to park overnight at this abandoned strip mall and didn't want anymore conflict with the Milpitas police so I parked out of view in the dark back alley of the strip mall next to a creepy old dumpster full of junk and spider webs. On the ground an array of broken liquor bottles, empty beer cans, and trash added to the graveyard ambiance, but at least the police wouldn't see us in this dark creepy alley and that was the main thing.

I began to prepare Lady and I for bed, but in the light of the full moon I noticed something very odd in the dumpster that caught my eye. There was a dark human shape protruding out of the dumpster and at first I assumed it was a broken discarded mannequin and casually went back to preparing Lady and I for bed.

But every so often I would glance back at the dumpster and got the creepy feeling that *wasn't* a mannequin. But if it wasn't a mannequin *what* the hell was it??? I started to imagine all kinds of things. Maybe it was a *dead* body! Maybe someone got murdered and the murderer dumped the *dead* body in this dumpster and I'm the first one to see it!

I should get out and look, but I was already half undressed for bed, and it was probably all just my imagination. So I went back to preparing Lady and I for bed and tried to forget about it, but I couldn't forget about it, and every so often I would glance back at the figure in the dumpster and my gut kept telling me . . .

Something is wrong here.
Something is very, very, wrong here.

Just then the figure in the dumpster started to move in a very slow and creepy manner. *Holy shit!!! What the fuck???* Then it turned its head slowly and the light of the full moon lit up its face and its face was hideous and grotesque*!!!* Whatever this damn thing was is wasn't *human!!!*

I quickly fired up *The Black Bat* and got us the hell out of there *fast* which jarred Lady awake.

"Huh??? What??? What's goin' on, Mr. Man*???* Why are we leaving*???"*

"I decided this wasn't such a good spot afterall."

"It looked good to me."

"Yeah, well, you didn't see what I saw."

"Whad-ya *see?"*

"Nothin'."

"You said you saw somethin'."

"I changed my mind. I didn't see anything."

"You saw *something*, Mr. Man, out with it."

"I told you; it was *nothing*."

"If it was *nothing* why are we leaving?"

"Just drop it Lady. You don't wanna know."

"Why don't I wanna know?"

"You don't even wanna know why you don't wanna know."

"That bad?"

"Worse."

"What was it?"

"I don't wanna talk about it."

"You saw some creepy ass *shit???*"

"Worse than creepy ass shit."

"*Worse* than creepy ass shit??? What could be *worse* than creepy ass shit???"

"A Dumpster Demon."

"You saw a Dumpster Demon???"

"Yeah."

"How do you know it was a Dumpster Demon???"

"It was in the fucking *dumpster.*"

"How do you know it was a *demon?*"

"It wasn't *human.*"

"What did it look like?"

"It looked like a charbroiled *corpse*."

"*Eeeww!!!*"

"*Major Eeeww.*"

"Why didn't you *kill it!*"

"Kill *it???* Kill it with *what???*"

"I don't know. You're the *parapsychologist*. Don't you know how to kill a Dumpster Demon*???*"

"No. I *don't*. I didn't receive any training on Dumpster Demons. I didn't even know Dumpster Demons *existed* until a few minutes ago. Besides, I don't think you can't *kill* a Dumpster Demon."

"Why *not???*"

"I'm pretty sure they're already *dead*."

"Like a *zucchini???*"

"Zombie."

"I *said* that."

"That's right, Lady; like a *zombie*."

"There must be some way to kill 'em, Mr. Man."

"Nope."

"What is we drop an atomic bomb on his head?"

"Where are we gonna get an *atomic bomb???*"

"The army surplus store."

"They don't have atomic bombs."

"They *don't???*"

"No. They only sell things like canteens, compasses, and boots."

"*Canteens, compasses,* and *boots???* We can't kill the Dumpster Demon with *canteens, compasses, and boots!!!*"

"I know."

"The army surplus store sucks donkey dicks!!!"

"Relax, Lady. You're all wound up."

"I wanna kill the Dumpster Demon."

"Not gonna happen Lady. Just let it go."

    Lady is very disappointed and releases a heavy sigh.

"Mr. Man???"

"Yeah?"

"Where do Dumpster Demons come from???"

"They come from the deep dark catacombs of *Naraka*."

"What are the deep dark catacombs of *Bakaka???*"

"*Naraka.*"

"I *said* that."

"*Naraka* is the Buddhist word for the vast limitless regions of *Hell.*"

"So, Dumpster Demons come from *Hell???*"

"Yes, Lady. They come from Hell."

"Do they have dumpsters in Hell?"

"I don't know."

"If his home is Hell *why* is he *here???*"

"I don't know."

"*How* did he get *here???*"

"I don't know."

"*Why* do Dumpster Demons like *dumpsters???*"

"I don't know."

"How do Dumpster Demons *become* Dumpster Demons*???*"

"I don't know."

"Do Dumpster Demons *eat???*"

"Lady, if you ask me *one* more question I'm trading you in for a *dog!!!*"

"I'm sorry, Mr. Man; but I can't stop thinking about Dumpster Demons."

"I see that and it *concerns* me."

"Why*???*"

"Remember what I taught you about *The Law of Attraction?*"

"*The Law of Attraction??? The Law of Attraction??? The Law of Attraction.* Oh, yeah*!!!* I remember*!!!* That was somethin' about somethin,' *right???*"

"Listen Lady, *The Law of Attraction* is very simple:

You attract what you think about.

"Isn't that what I just *said???*"

"All I'm saying is, if you go around *thinking* about Dumpster Demons you're gonna attract Dumpster Demons."

"So *what* should I think about then*???*"

"You should think about something *nice, pleasant, cheerful,* and *wholesome.*"

"Like *what???*"

"Oh, I don't know; how about *butterflies* and *green meadows.*"

"*Butterflies* and *green meadows???*"

"Yeah."

"So if I go around thinking about *butterflies* and *green meadows* I'll *attract* butterflies and green meadows???"

"Absolutely."

"Okay Mr. Man I'll *do* it."

"Good girl Lady."

Lady suddenly gazes out the window quizzically.

"*Ummm,* Mr. Man???"

"Yeah?"

"*Where* are we *going???*"

"I have no fucking clue; is there any beer left?"

DON'T GO IN THERE

After the Dumpster Demon incident Lady and I left Milpitas for good and relocated back to Cupertino just in time for the start of the 2020 COVID LOCKDOWN. Lady and I quickly made the Monta Vista High School student parking lot our "Base Camp" because the school was closed for the lockdown and I figured the cops wouldn't bother us there. I was now *back* at my old high school, not as a *winner*, but as a homeless *loser* living in his car with his cat and I wondered what my old high school classmates would think if they saw me now.

The best part of living at the high school parking lot was the fluorescent green porta potty that conveniently serviced all my #1 and #2 needs. I used that porta potty for weeks without incident. Then one day all that *changed*. I entered the porta potty as usual, sat on the seat, and began doing some #2 business when I suddenly felt a strange *tingling* sensation on my penis. *Hmmm.* I never felt that before. It was early morning and I wasn't quite awake yet, so I just wrote it off as my imagination and immediately the tingling *disappeared.* But a few seconds later the *tingling* returned on my penis and I thought, *What the hell???* But once again I chalked it up to my imagination and once again the tingling sensation on my penis *disappeared.* I finished my #2 business and walked back to the car, but the Sherlock Holmes in my head wanted to solve the mystery and so I went back to the porta potty with a flashlight and my reading glasse. I then shone the flashlight into the bowels and nether regions of the porta potty and got the shock of my life. *Ants everywhere!!!* It *wasn't* my imagination . . .

PORTA POTTY ANTS
PARTIED ON MY PENIS ! ! !

The ants were a *new* addition to the porta potty and the Sherlock Holmes in my head wanted to know <u>WHY</u> they were here <u>NOW</u> and not before. I knew from Newtonian physics that every <u>EFFECT</u> has a <u>CAUSE</u> and so I looked for the *cause* of this *effect* and there is was . . .

A bag of McDonald's leftovers floating in the porta potty.

Yep, some *asshole, dickhead, scumbucket, douchebag, loser, creep-a-zoid, dildo, piece-of-shit, retarded dumbass bitch* ruined the porta potty for EVERYONE by heinously tossing a bag of McDonald's leftovers into the porta potty which then became a powerful *magnet* for all the ants in the area and which now takes us to . . .

Ant Psychology 101

JACK the ANT. Hey Joe. Joe!

JOE the ANT. What?

JACK. Come here.

JOE. What is it?

JACK. Come here!

JOE. What?

JACK. Bag of McDonald's leftovers in the porta potty.

JOE. No way.

JACK. *Way—Look!*

JOE. Holy *shit!*

JACK. I told you.

JOE. Sound the alarm! Call the crew! Invite the girls! The party is on *! ! !*

SIMON the ANT. What party? What are you guys talkin' about?

JOE. There's a bag of McDonald's leftovers in the porta potty.

SIMON. Yeah, so*???*

JOE. You ain't never had McDonald's leftovers soaked in porta potty chems and poop before*???*

SIMON. No.

JACK. How old are you boy?

SIMON. Five weeks old.

JACK. Look here whippersnapper. Tain't nuttin' better in this evil world than a bag of McDonald's leftovers soaked in porta potty chems and poop.

SIMON. Better than crusty old dog shit on the side of the road*???*

JACK. Way better.

JOE. Tonight we're gonna party like there's no tomorrow.

SIMON. Can I come?

JOE. Hell yeah, you can come.

JACK. The playboy bunny ants will probably show up. 'Dem honey bunnies is *wild*. You play your cards right tonight boy and you'll wake up a *man* tomorrow.

THE ONE

There isn't much to do at night when you live in a car with your cat so I would think about THE ONE a lot.

"You're thinking about her again Mr. Man."

"I know."

"It doesn't do any good to think about her."

"I know."

"You only get depressed thinking about her."

"I know."

"You messed up. That's all."

"I know."

"She's gone."

"I know."

"You gotta stop thinkin' about her."

"I know."

"She's not comin' back."

"I know."

"Not in this life. Maybe in another life."

"I hope so."

"But it won't be easy."

"How so?"

"Well, let's say you meet again in another life."

"Yeah."

"What if she's married or happily coupled."

"*Damn.*"

"You didn't think about that, did you."

"No, I didn't."

"You fucked up."

"I know."

"You see Mr. Man, it would have been a lot better if you hadn't fucked up, but you fucked up, so now it's gonna be hard for you guys to get back together even in another life."

"Shit."

"It could take many lifetimes for you guys to meet and get back together again."

"I'm a fuckin' idiot."

"Well, I won't argue with that, Mr. Man."

"I see what you mean, Lady. It could take *hundreds* or *thousands* of years for us to get back together again."

"That's *true*, Mr. Man, but what is *Time* when you love someone?"

"Good point, Lady. How do you know so much about *love???*"

"I've been in love a few times Mr. Man. I never did anything as *stupid* as you did, but I've been in love enough times to know that it's time for you to let THE ONE go and get on with your life."

"Yeah. You're *right*, Lady. Gotta let her go. Gotta get on with the rest of my life."

"That's the *spirit*, Mr. Man. You don't have time to think about *her* right now anyway."

"I *don't?*"

"Wake up and smell the coffee Mr. Man*!!!* We're livin' in a car*!!!*"

"Right . . . you're *right* . . . I know."

"You know what your *problem* is Mr. Man???"

"What???"

"You're a *Dreamer*."

"That's a *bad* thing???"

"It's a bad thing when you're livin' in your car with your cat!"

"You're *right*, Lady. I'm a *Dreamer*. I've been a *Dreamer* my entire life. And where has it gotten me? *Nowhere*."

I suddenly became very sad.

"You're a good man, Mr. Man. But the time has come to rise to the occasion and get us out of this homeless mess."

"How am I gonna do that???"

"I don't know. You're a talented dude, Mr. Man. You'll think of somethin'. All you gotta do is focus and get your drinking down to a reasonable level."

"My drinking *is* down to a reasonable level."

Lady raised an eyebrow and glared at me.

"Alright," I sighed. "I'll cut down on my drinking."

A good woman always brings out the best in a man—even if that good woman is a cat.

THE DOME
OF DESTINY

Three weeks later I was sleeping in the car with Lady as usual when sometime in the middle of the night I suddenly found myself seated inside a white marble gazebo situated in the center of a vast and brilliant green lawn under the clearest blue sky I have ever seen. Dotted around the landscape here and there were bright and colorful pyramids, domes, and other striking architecture that strictly adhered to the sacred geometry of *Metatron's Cube*. Off in the distance were mighty snow capped mountains and crags of Himalayan grandeur. It was all quite breathtaking and I assumed it was just a dream.

I then noticed a very regal looking man walking briskly toward me with an elegant walking stick. He wore a dark leather top hat with laces, a long stylized violet coat, dark stripped pants, and knee high boots with buckles. He had short dark hair and a neatly manicured beard and mustache. He had the look and aura of an *artiste*, *philosopher*, or *nobleman* about him. As he drew closer his captivating blue eyes radiated enormous power, wisdom, warmth, and good cheer. He was, of course, *The Professor.*

"Hello Z!" he boomed like a hearty ship captain.

"Greetings Professor," I replied. "*Where* am I*???*"

"You're in *Shambhala*," he smiled.

[In Buddhism and Theosophy "Shambhala" is a secret astral world of avatars, ascended masters, and spirit guides accessible only through a secret interdimensional portal located somewhere in the Himalayan mountains.]

"Why am I *here*, Professor*???*"

"I summoned you here."

"For *what* purpose*???*"

Just then The Professor's piercing blue eyes suddenly became laser sharp and I knew he was about to tell me something very important.

"As you know, your *first* mission was a failure because you failed to heed my warning and nearly got yourself killed."

I nodded.

"Fortunately, your *second* mission was a complete success."

I nodded again.

"I summoned you here today to give you your *third* and *final* mission."

"*Third* mission*???* I only signed up for *two* missions."

"*The Great Council* is graciously offering you a *third* mission and thus the opportunity to redeem yourself for your *failed* mission. However, if you would prefer to accept the failure on your cosmic record then your starseed mission is complete and you can go home now."

Nope. I didn't want any "failures" on my cosmic record. Doesn't look good and makes me ineligible for promotions and highly sought after assignments. Nevertheless, I knew the third mission would be a very difficult one and so I asked with great trepidation . . .

"What's the *third* mission*???*"

"Come with me," The Professor said and we walked across the vast green lawn toward a white geometric dome off in the distance. The dome was approximately 100 feet tall and 100 feet wide. When we got to the entrance two gold doors lasered with strange hieroglyphics silently opened and beckoned us in . . .

"What is *this* place*???*" I asked.

"*The Dome of Destiny*," The Professor replied.

"*The Dome of Destiny???* What are we gonna do here*???*"

"You'll see."

I followed The Professor inside and the interior of the dome was a strange sight to behold. There were rows and rows of black video screens from floor to ceiling and 360 degrees around. In the center of the dome was a single rotating chair that allowed one to view all the video screens quickly and easily. The Professor silently motioned me to sit in the chair and then The Professor disappeared into thin air as he often does.

I was all alone in the dome now and felt a bit queasy. I had the overwhelming feeling that something BIG was about to happen but exactly WHAT I had no idea. A moment later the dome darkened and all the video screens lit up and came to life.

What happened next was a shock of galactic magnitude. Every video screen began to play "highlights" from my past lives!!! All my incarnations played out before me in rapid succession on rows and rows of video screens.

I quickly saw that *none* of my past lives were on Earth. *All* of my past lives were in the Pleiades star system. This explained why people usually regarded me as *different, enigmatic,* and a bit *strange.* Not only was I from another planet; I was from another star system!!!

I noticed in the video highlights that Pleiadians followed a *cosmic religion* that was similar to *Buddhism* insofar as the immediate goal of this cosmic religion was *Self-Improvement* and the ultimate goal *Moksha.*

I further saw in the video clips that by age five Pleiadian children had already mastered *telepathy* and understood the purpose of *reincarnation* so well that it was quite common to hear a 5-year-old in the Pleiades say something like,

"In past lives I mastered A, B, and C, and now I'm back to work on X, Y, and Z."

A 5-year-old in the Pleiades is already light-years ahead of adult Earthlings in *psychic* and *spiritual* development. But the *biggest* and *greatest* shock of all was *Lady* was in most of my past lives*!!!* In the Pleiades Lady was often our family cat or my personal cat, and that explained the powerful, strange, and eerie *"connection"* I felt with Lady when we met that fateful day in the summer of 2004.

At that point all the video screens faded to BLACK except ONE screen. The final screen played a video clip of what appeared to be my *future* and showed me typing away on a laptop computer day after day in the car with Lady.

That was *weird*. I had no plans to write anything *new* and I certainly wouldn't attempt to write anything living in the car with Lady. That would be *way* too hard. Then the final screen faded to BLACK and the house lights came back up.

The Professor reappeared out of thin air and glibly asked, "Well? Did you enjoy the show?"

I was speechless. All I could think to say was,"*What* was I writing in the car?"

"Your *magnum opus.*"

"My *magnum opus???*"

"Your *magnum opus* is your *third* mission."

"What's it about???"

"On the surface it's about a man living in his car with his cat; below the surface it's about the *meaning* and *purpose* of life."

"I dunno Professor. I'm tired and depressed. I don't think I could write a book right now, much less my *magnum opus.*"

"Do you still want to train at [1]OMA?"

My eyes suddenly opened wide like a kid in a candy store. The biggest of all my big dreams was to train at OMA and become a Spirit Guide like The Professor—complete with Spirit Guide *super powers!!!*

"Of course," I replied.

"Write this book and you begin training at OMA at the end of this life."

Holy. Fuckin'. Shit.

By my own estimation I was a few starseed missions away from being worthy of OMA, but now The Professor is telling me all I have to do is write *this* book and I'm *in!!!*

"Well*???* What do you say*???*"

"I'll *do* it," I said.

---

[1] *Order of Melchizedek Academy*

MY MAGNUM OPUS

On the morning of April 22, 2020, I awoke, rubbed the sleep from my eyes, and psyched myself up for the monumental task of writing *"THE GAME of LIFE"* living in my car with my cat and feeling like total fucking shit.

And so I said aloud to the gods and the universe, *"Today I begin writing my magnum opus and I am filled with a sense of awe and responsibility."* That helped a little, but not much, so I said it again, "*Today I begin writing my magnum opus and I am filled with a sense of awe and responsibility.*" That felt a little better, but I still needed more inspiration so I said it several more times with feeling, "*Today I begin writing my magnum opus and I am filled with a sense of awe and responsibility.*" Lady was sleeping and began to toss and turn from all the noise I was making. Meanwhile, I was getting really psyched up and repeated the line several more times for good luck, "*Today I begin writing my magnum opus and I am filled with a sense of awe and responsibility.*"

Lady opened one eye, yawned, and said,

"What are you *babbling* about Mr. Man*???*"

"Today I begin writing my *magnum opus* and I am filled with a sense of awe and responsibility."

"What's a *magnum octopus???*"

"Magnum *opus.*"

"I *said* that."

"A *magnum opus* is a writer's greatest work. The work that towers above all his other works. The work he will be most remembered for. The work that secures his place in the pantheon of literature."

"You woke me up for *that???*"

"I thought you might wanna know."

"Mr. Man, how many times have I told you not to wake me up unless there's *food* involved."

"Sorry."

"What's this *magnum octopus* about anyway*???*"

"It's about you and me living in the car."

"Why didn't you say so in the first place. I can see it now. I'm gonna be the Rockstar of this *magnum octopus.*"

"The *Rockstar???*"

"Listen Mr. Man, what this *magnum octopus* needs is a lead with Rockstar X Factor and lots of it. That's where I come in. I was born with Rockstar X Factor. I drip Rockstar X Factor. Readers are gonna need a mop and bucket to mop up all the Rockstar X Factor I'm gonna drip all over the pages of this *magnum octopus.*"

"*Magnum opus.*"

"I said that."

"But I'm the *writer* of the book."

"Writer *schmiter* Mr. Man. Anyone can write a book. That's the easy part. It's a lot harder to bring massive Rockstar X Factor to the table."

Then Lady stared out the window all dreamy eyed . . .

"I can see it now. I'm gonna be *huge*. My face is gonna be on TV, video games, T-shirts, coffee cups, lunch bags, and cereal boxes all over the world. Step aside Scooby-Doo. Lady Le Mans is cooler than you . . ."

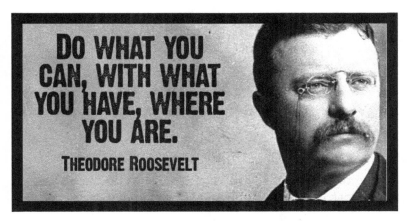

DO WHAT YOU CAN, WITH WHAT YOU HAVE, WHERE YOU ARE.

THEODORE ROOSEVELT

I BEGIN WRITING

Writing *"The Game of Life"* was no easy task. For one thing I didn't have a computer so I drove to the public library and checked out a *Chromebook* with my library card. The timing was *auspicious*. The very next day *ALL* California public libraries closed for an entire year during the COVID-19 LOCKDOWN and I got to keep the Chromebook for an entire year. Had I gone to the library *one* day later you would not be reading this book because there would be no book. Nevertheless, getting a Chromebook from the public library was the *easy* part of writing this book. Try writing a book living in your car with your cat during a GLOBAL PANDEMIC LOCKDOWN and let me know how that goes for you.

Here now for your entertainment pleasure is what a typical day writing *"The Game of Life"* was like . . .

A Typical Day Writing
"THE GAME of LIFE"

7:00AM

I wake up, get dressed, make my car bed, brush Lady, clean Lady's litter box, and drive to a public restroom to poop, pee, and wash my face.

8:00AM

I drive to a local gas station, get some gas, and a big cup of plain black coffee because *real* men drink plain black coffee.

8:20AM

I drive to a local market and get Lady's cat food.

8:30AM

I park at Monta Vista High School or Blackberry Farm, feed Lady, take one sip of my gas station coffee, open the Chromebook, and begin writing for the day . . .

BAARRFF ! ! !

8:35AM

Lady has just thrown up in the car. I've only written ONE fucking sentence and already I have to STOP writing and clean up a massive mass of warm sticky cat vomit. It takes 30 minutes to clean up the massive mass of warm sticky cat vomit which puts me in a really BAD mood. Writing is ridiculously hard even when you're in a GOOD mood and almost *impossible* when you're in a BAD mood. And now I'm in a BAD mood. I reach for my coffee hoping a few sips of hot coffee will give me a quick "reset" so I can resume writing at a high level. I take a gulp of coffee and *cringe*. The coffee is now cold and flat.

9:20AM
I get 20 minutes of writing in then—

WHUURRRRR ! ! !

Fuck me! The groundskeeper has begun cleaning the grounds with a leaf blower and is very close to me. No way in hell can I write with that goddamn noise blasting my head so I start the car and relocate to nearby Kennedy Middle School. I connect the Chromebook to the parking lot Wi-Fi and get 10 minutes of writing in when—

WHUURRRRR ! ! !

Fuck my bitch ass ! ! ! The groundskeeper here has begun to clean the grounds with a leaf blower 20 feet away. Moving here was totally pointless and I have to move again.

9:45AM
I relocate to *"The Oaks Shopping Center,"* connect the Chromebook to the parking lot Wi-Fi, and resume writing. I get 15 minutes of writing in then—

HONK ! ! ! BEEP ! ! ! HONK ! ! !

BEEP ! ! ! HONK ! ! ! BEEP ! ! !

HONK ! ! ! BEEP ! ! ! HONK ! ! !

BEEP ! ! ! HONK ! ! ! BEEP ! ! !

HONK ! ! ! BEEP ! ! ! HONK ! ! !

A car alarm has gone off in the parking lot and won't stop. Where the hell is the *owner???* Doesn't he hear *it???* No one comes to turn off the car alarm and it keeps going and going and going like the Energizer Bunny. I'm fucked and have to relocate—*again!*

10:00AM

I relocate to the Cupertino public library, connect the Chromebook to the parking lot Wi-Fi, and resume writing. I get 10 minutes of writing in then—

BLAP ! ! ! BLAP ! ! ! BLAP ! ! !

BLAP ! ! ! BLAP ! ! ! BLAP ! ! !

BLAP ! ! ! BLAP ! ! ! BLAP ! ! !

BLAP ! ! ! BLAP ! ! ! BLAP ! ! !

A nearby road crew begins jackhammering the road and I'm *fucked* again.

10:30AM

This time I relocate to nearby *"Monta Vista Park"* on Foothill Blvd. I connect the Chromebook to the parking lot Wi-Fi and resume writing. I get 10 minutes of writing in when a complete stranger in an old truck pulls up along side me and motions for me to roll my window down. This happens all the time and the random stranger usually says something massively stupid like . . .

STRANGER. Is that a Dodge Dart*???*

"The Black Bat" looks *nothing* like a Dodge Dart and this guy is a complete idiot. Unfortunately, my 1966 Corvair is a magnet for complete idiots.

Here now for your entertainment pleasure are the <u>Top 10 Comments</u> random strangers have made on my 1966 Corvair.

TOP 10 COMMENTS

- What year is your *Camero?*

- Nice *Nova.*

- Is that a *Celica?*

- Sweet *Mustang* bro.

- Is that a *Chevelle?*

- Wow, I haven't seen a *Vega* in 30 years.

- Is that a *Dodge Dart?* (3 times!!!)

- Does your *Mazda* have the rotary engine?

- Is that the *Datsun* 240z or 260z?

- *(old hippie chick)* Cool *Karmen Gia!*

<u>11:00AM</u>
Dodge Dart idiot departs and I get a full hour of writing in which feels like an hour of hot steamy sex with a *Hooters Girl* in the back seat of my car.

<u>12 NOON</u>
It is now 12 noon and time for lunch. Lunch is always something *cheap* 'cuz I'm a poor unemployed writer living in my car with my cat. Here's a typical lunch week . . .

<u>(MONDAY)</u>
Hot, ready-made pizza slices from 7-Eleven.
(Cheap, but taste like cardboard.)

(TUESDAY)
The current 2-for1 deal at Jack in the Box.
(Everything at Jack in the Box tastes great!)

(WEDNESDAY)
The Subway sandwich meal deal
(includes a drink and bag of chips!)

(THURSDAY)
A big bag of donut holes that will be my
breakfast, lunch, and dinner all day.
(Tasty & cheap!)

(FRIDAY)
The Little Caesars lunch special for $4.99
(Tasty and cheap. Little Caesars rocks!)

(SATURDAY)
A bag of odds and ends from the supermarket
(e.g., red licorice, a cheese bagel, a glazed donut, a mini bag of potato chips, mozzarella sticks, and a nectarine. Hmmm, sound familiar???)

(SUNDAY)
Sunday I'm back at Jack in the Box
('cuz everything at Jack in the Box tastes great!)

1:00PM
Lunch is over and I must get back to work, so I return to the Monta Vista High School parking lot to write. The groundskeeper is gone, all is quiet, and I resume writing my *magnum opus*. I get 30 minutes of writing in then—

NOOOOOOO ! ! !

THE SKATEBOARDERS ARE BACK

Six annoying as fuck skateborders who think the parking lot is their very own private skate park where they can practice their moves, holler and scream like psychos in a psyche ward and disrupt the delicate writing process of an award winning writer writing his *magnum opus*. There is a special place in Hell for these hideous abominations of misplaced sperm and I curse the maggot-infested wombs that bore these denizens of disturbance.

I am forced to relocate—again.

"Someday I'll get even with you skateboarders. Someday when you least expect it. I'll be there. And you'll be sorry." - Z. Z. Le Mans

1:45PM

Back at Kennedy Middle School all is quiet and I get into the "Writer's Zen Zone" fast and hard by quickly slamming two mini bottles of chardonnay. In 10 minutes I'm in the "Writer's Zen Zone" where I soar like an eagle in the rarified air of literature and get two full hours of uninterrupted writing in.

Many literary scholars frown on writers who write under the influence of alcohol. And many cops frown on writers who down copious amounts of chardonnay writing their *magnum opus* at the local high school. But for the record, let me state here and now an *indisputable* FACT:

"All the really great writers drank. Writers who don't drink are imposters, hacks, and prudes." - Z. Z. Le Mans

3:45PM

It is now 3:45PM and I am *mentally* and *emotionally* exhausted. I quit writing for the day and relax by blasting some *Classic Rock* on the Chromebook and opening another mini bottle of chardonnay.

Cheers!

BUSTED AGAIN

"I see you checkin' out that hottie Mr. Man."

Busted again.

"Yeah, *so???*"

"So, she's out of your league."

"Whaddaya mean she's out of my league???"

"You're livin' in your car with your cat. *All* women are out of your league."

"Okay, you made your point. I can still have my mental fantasies can't I?"

Lady sighs and rolls her eyes.

"Mr. Man, you need to get your mind out of the gutter and focus on getting us a *home*."

"Yes, *Mom*."

"How's our *magnum octopus* coming along???"

"It's coming."

"You know, you could be working *harder* on that thing. At the rate you're goin' we'll be *dead* of old age before it's done."

"You can't rush great literature Lady. It's not like grinding sausage. A great book has to marinate, percolate, brew, stew, and simmer for a long period of time. And then there's months and months of rewriting and polishing to be done. Writing a book is a monumental task Lady. You can't write *'Moby Dick'* in a day."

"Sorry, Mr. Man. I didn't know you were writing a literary masterpiece. I thought you were writing a book about our day to day nefarious adventures."

"That can be a literary masterpiece; it depends on who's doing the writing. If I say so myself *"THE GAME of LIFE"* has *literary, spiritual, philosophical,* and *psychological* merit that readers will find beneficial to their lives."

"Didn't you write a chapter on the *Dumpster Demon???*"

"Yeah."

"How is that chapter *beneficial* to readers lives*???*"

"Isn't it *obvious???* That chapter warns readers not to park next to creepy ass dumpsters at night."

"Readers need a *book* for *that???*"

"Readers need our book for a lot of reasons, Lady. People look at us and think, *'Look at that poor bastard living in his car with his cat.'* But our homeless odyssey is actually a crash course in ESOTERIC ARTS & SCIENCES and illustrates how a kaleidoscope of existential, sociological, environmental, genetic, economic, psychological, metaphysical, and quantum mechanical *factors* affect and counter-affect each other in a Space/Time loop that determines a person's dharma, karma, past, present, and future."

WTF ? ? ?

"Somebody hand me a shovel; the shit's gettin' *thick* in here."

"Lady, maybe you should just concentrate on being a *cat* and not try to grasp concepts, theories, and theorems light-years beyond your cat brain comprehension."

"*Hmmft!* I know when I've been insulted. I'm going to my cat cave to take my morning nap. Be a good man and have my lunch ready at the *correct* time today and not *twenty* minutes late like it was yesterday."

TYPING & TALKING

I'm typing away on this book, and for reasons unknown, whenever I'm typing away on this book Lady likes to chat me up . . .

"Mr. Man?"

"Yeah?"

"Do you ever regret taking me in?"

"Yeah."

"No, I'm *serious.*"

"Yeah."

"When???"

"When you *vomit* all over the car."

"That can't be helped; I have a *sensitive* stomach."

"You don't *chew* your food."

"I have a *sensitive* stomach."

"You don't *chew* your food."

"I have a *sensitive* stomach."

"It's a *chewing* issue."

"It's a *stomach* issue."

"It's a *chewing* issue."

"It's a *stomach* issue."

"*Chewing* issue!"

"*Stomach* issue!"

"*Chewing* issue!"

"*Stomach* issue!"

"*Chewing!*"

"*Stomach!*"

"*Chewing!*"

"*Stomach!*"

Ugh ! ! ! ! !

"Mr. Man, we're never gonna *agree* on this are we."

"Nope."

"Well, let me put it another way. When I'm not vomiting all over the car I'm your pride and joy, *right???*"

"Yep."

"Thought so. Just wanted to hear you say it. *Whoa! Look at the time!* I'm late for my afternoon nap."

Lady sashays and slithers through the door of her cat cave to take her afternoon nap.

"*Oh,* Mr. Man."

"Yeah?"

"One more thing."

"Yeah?"

"Don't wake me unless there's *food* involved."

mettle

The dictionary defines "mettle" as,

A person's ability to cope well with difficulties and face demanding situations in a spirited and resilient way.

Mettle is the #1 thing you need in life. If you have sufficient mettle you will concur life. If you lack sufficient mettle life will concur you. It's that simple.

Even spoiled brat *3rd-Basers* need mettle because their parents' money and influence will only take them so far in life and then they will need mettle just like the rest of us.

In *The Game of Life* there are winners, losers, bench warmers, people with dreams, people who gave up on their dreams, people who never had any dreams, people who settled for less and now regret it, people crippled by addictions of one type or another, and the more than 700,000 people who commit suicide every year because *The Game of Life* is just too damn *hard!*

But *The Game of Life* is not about giving up on your dreams or giving up on life *altogether*—it's about <u>IMPROVING YOUR GAME</u>*!!!* And anyone can improve their *game.* Baseball players do it all the time—that's why they take batting practice.

Like baseball players, you need to work on your *game* in *The Game of Life.* This is where 50% of people drop the ball. 50% of people are too lazy, too unmotivated, too cowardly, too anxious, too crippled by doubt, too confused, too pampered, too spoiled, too lost in addiction, or too stuck in their "comfort zone" to work on their *game* in *The Game of Life.*

And they have no one to blame but themselves.

One of my lifelong hobbies has been to read *"Poor Man Success Stories"* and analyze what all these poor *nobodies* did to become hugely successful in life.

I figured they must know a "secret" I didn't.

Like Sherlock Holmes I looked for the *secret* that took these poor *nobodies* from rags to riches. And I *found* it! I found their *secret!* But the shocker was their *secret* wasn't much of a *secret.* In fact, I can summarize their *secret* in just three words . . .

Never Give Up!

THE GAME OF LIFE

Roar of the Crowd

JOE GARAGIOLA. Well Tony, it doesn't look good for Mr. Man and Lady.

TONY KUBEK. No Joe, it sure doesn't. Bottom of the 9th inning, bases loaded, two outs, and Mr. Man and Lady are down by three in *The Game of Life*.

JOE. It'll take a grand slam to win it and Mr. Man will be facing Roger Clemens.

ROGER CLEMENS. *The meanest most ruthless pitcher in baseball history. Known for his 98 mph fastball, hostile personality, steroid controversies, and throwing at batters' heads!!! A real motherfucker.*

JOE. Tony, what's the scouting report on Mr. Man?

TONY. The scouting report on Mr. Man is he played some vacant lot baseball as a kid and once led the vacant lot league in home runs.

JOE. Vacant lot baseball, *eh?* And now he's going up against Roger Clemens at Yankee Stadium. This should be interesting, Tony.

TONY. I have a feeling it will be.

Buddha is on third base, Freud is on second base, and The Professor is on first base.

Legendary Yankee third baseman Alex "A-Rod" Rodriguez looks Buddha up and down with amusement.

A-ROD. Dude, are you really the *Buddha???*

Buddha chuckles.

BUDDHA. Dude, are you really the 3rd baseman.

Yankee second baseman Bobby Richardson eyes Freud with great admiration.

RICHARDSON. This is a great honor, sir. I minored in psych and wrote my final term paper on your *"Oedipus theory."*

Freud nods politely and puffs on his cigar.

RICHARDSON. Doctor, maybe you can help me. I keep having recurring dreams about the Lady in Red.

FREUD. Zee Lady in Vred???

RICHARDSON. She stands at the foot of my bed in a red dress. Her left eye is normal but her right eye is a clock face. She has no nose and where her mouth should be is written the word *"sinep"* in black eyeliner.

FREUD. Jes. Many of my pazients zee dat verd in dair dreams.

RICHARDSON. What does it mean, doctor?

FREUD. *"Sinep"* is penis spelled backwards. Psychoanalysis has proven time and time again that all neuroses and psychoses have a sexual origin.

Freud pulls out his wallet and hands Richardson his business card.

FREUD. Coalz my zecretary in zee morning. Ve'll get to zee bottom of zis "Vwooman in Vred."

RICHARDSON. Thank you, doctor.

The Professor stands on first base looking very out of place and otherworldly. Yankees first baseman Anthony Rizzo eyes The Professor quizzically up and down not sure what to make of him.

RIZZO. *Who* are you supposed to be*???*

PROFESSOR. I'm *The Professor.*

RIZZO. *The Professor???* How do you figure into all of this*???*

PROFESSOR. I'm Mr. Man's spirit guide.

RIZZO. *Spirit guide???* Is this game a dream or *what???*

PROFESSOR. The whole of life is a dream.

Mr. Man steps into the batter's box wearing faded blue jeans, a faded blue T-shirt, and NO helmet.

PLATE UMPIRE. This is Roger Clemens, Mr. Man. I'd wear a batting helmet if I were you.

MR. MAN. I'm from the vacant lot league ump. I've never worn a batting helmet in my life. I'm not gonna start now.

PLATE UMPIRE. Suit yourself; it's your funeral.

Mr. Man surveys the intimidating scene before him, reaches into his back pocket, pulls out a mini bottle of chardonnay, and unscrews the cap.

PLATE UMPIRE. What's *that* Mr. Man???

MR. MAN. It's a mini bottle of chardonnay from 7-Eleven.

PLATE UMPIRE. Mr. Man, there's no chardonnay in baseball*!*

MR. MAN. There is now.

Mr. Man takes a swig of chardonnay, returns the bottle to his back pocket, digs his feet into the batter's box, and takes a few check swings.

TONY. Looks like we're ready to go.

JOE. Boy, look at that 'stare down' Clemens is giving Mr. Man.

TONY. Classic Clemens. *Intimidation* is half his game.

JOE. Clemens takes the sign from Posada and goes into his windup. Here's the pitch. Swing and a miss. Strike one.

TONY. Vicious cut by Mr. Man.

JOE. He's swingin' for the fences, Tony.

TONY. He has to. A base hit won't do it.

JOE. Clemens looks in for the sign. Here comes the pitch. Swing and a miss. The count is now 0 and 2 and Mr. Man has hit nothin' but air.

TONY. Mr. Man has shown a lot of courage here, but it takes more than courage to play major league baseball.

JOE. Both men ready now. This could be the last pitch of the game. Clemens takes the sign from Posada. Here's the pitch.

CRACK!!!

JOE. Deep drive down the left field line! Way back! Way back! Going! Going! *FOUL!* Foul Ball! Holy Toledo! Mr. Man just took Roger Clemens 360 feet down the left field line!

TONY. That's gotta shake Clemens up a bit Joe.

JOE. I'll say. Mr. Man just showed everyone in Yankee Stadium he has the power to hit one outta here.

Freud casually tosses his cigar butt on the infield.

The Crowd Chuckles

2ND BASE UMPIRE. Time out *! ! !*

The 2nd base umpire picks up Freud's cigar butt.

2ND BASE UMPIRE. Dr. Freud, you can't toss cigar butts on the infield of Yankee Stadium.

FREUD. And vie *not?* Iz just *dirt.*

2ND BASE UMPIRE. With all due respect doctor, this isn't Austria.

FREUD. *Hmmft.* That's obvious.

The cigar butt is taken off the field and the game resumes.

TONY. Mr. Man steps back into the batter's box.

JOE. Clemens looks in for the sign from Posada, goes into his windup, and here's the pitch . . .

The Crowd Gasps

JOE. Whoa*!!!* Clemens almost took Mr. Man's head off with that pitch*!!!*

TONY. Mr. Man barely got out of the way of that one.

JOE. Mr. Man gets up slowly and dusts himself off.

TONY. Look at the stare Mr. Man is giving Roger Clemens. I don't think Mr. Man was too happy with that last pitch.

JOE. Not at all. Mr. Man steps slowly back into the batter's box and takes a few check swings. One and one is the count to Mr. Man. Clemens takes the sign and delivers the pitch . . .

CRACK*!!!*

JOE. Deep drive down the right field line! Way back! Way back! Going! Going! *FOUL!* Foul Ball! Holy Toledo! Mr. Man just took Roger Clemens 360 feet down the right field line!

TONY. You know Joe, I get the feeling Mr. Man can hit.

JOE. Whatever gave you that idea.

Shaken, Clemens goes nervously to the rosin bag to collect himself.

TONY. Clemens looks a bit shaken.

JOE. He sure does.

TONY. Mr. Man returns to the batter's box and takes a few check swings. The count remains 1 and 2 to Mr. Man.

JOE. Clemens takes the sign from Posada. Here's the pitch . . .

The Crowd Gasps

JOE. Whoa*!!!* Clemens almost took off Mr. Man's head *again!!!*

TONY. Mr. Man picks himself up off the ground and dusts himself off.

JOE. And now Mr. Man is saying something to Clemens.

TONY. And now Clemens is saying something back to Mr. Man.

JOE. Clemens and Mr. Man exchanging some heated words down on the field.

TONY. Things are really heating up between them.

JOE. They sure are. And now Mr. Man is walking out to the mound with the bat!!!

The Crowd Goes Wild ! ! !

JOE. Holy Toledo!!! Mr. Man is walking out to the mound with the bat!!!

TONY. Several Yankee players tackle Mr. Man to the ground.

JOE. And now Lady Le Mans comes charging out of the dugout baring her claws and fangs!!!

TONY. It's gonna get ugly, Joe!!!

Lady attacks the Yankee players that have Mr. Man pinned to the ground and the Yankee players scatter like flies, their uniforms torn to shreds.

"DANDY" the goofy New York Yankees mascot.

TONY. And now Dandy waddles in and clobbers Lady over the head with his big foam bat*!!!*

JOE. I don't think that was a good idea, Tony.

TONY. I don't think so either, Joe.

In two seconds Lady turns Dandy's bat into a pile of confetti and then bites Dandy in the butt ! ! !

Eee-Yow !!!

JOE. And now Freud is down*!!!* 83-year-old Sigmund Freud is down and down *hard* on the Yankee infield*!!!*

TONY. During the melee and confusion Derek Jeter accidentally backed into Freud and knocked him over.

Sorry for the accident Jeter tries to help Freud up and Freud clobbers Jeter over the head with his cane!!!

FREUD. Take zat you blundering *idziot!!!*

And now Yankee trainer Joe Forello trots onto the field to inspect Freud's injuries and Freud clobbers Forello over the head with his cane!!!

FREUD. Vee gone Zhankee horse doctor*!!!* I'm medical doctor from zee Unizverzity of Vienna*!!!*

TONY. And now some of the Yankee bench players are pushing and shoving *The Professor.*

JOE. He *din't* do anything. Holy Toledo*!!!* A Yankee player just sucker punched *The Professor* in the back of the head*!!!*

TONY. Dirty move*!*

JOE. All say. There was no call for that*!*

The Professor waves his mighty hand and all his Yankee attackers go flying end over end into the dugout.

CRASH!!!

JOE. Now second baseman Bobby Richardson is helping Freud back up on his feet.

RICHARDSON. I'm sorry doctor. Are you *okay???*

FREUD. I should have stayed in Austria. America is the land of Neanderthals, apes, and lunatics*!!!*

TONY. Freud is limping, Joe.

JOE. Freud clearly injured something in the fall.

TONY. And now Buddha has thrown up a peace sign. Buddha has thrown up a peace sign in an effort to restore peace here at Yankee Stadium.

JOE. I don't think a peace sign is gonna do it.

TONY. Not at Yankee Stadium.

Buddha's peace sign has no effect on the fight or the rowdy Yankee crowd.

BANG!!!

JOE. Holy mackerel*!!!* Buddha just got hit in the head by a beer bottle*!!!* A Yankee fan threw a beer bottle onto the field and it hit Buddha in the head*!!!*

TONY. That's *low* even by Yankee Stadium standards.

JOE. And now Buddha's head is bleeding*!!!*

Undaunted by the pain or blood Buddha holds his hands high in the air and solemnly utters these words...

BUDDHA. By the powers invested in me by Lord Metatron, Lord Melchizedek, Lord Ashtar, Lord Kumara, and Lord Maitreya, I command all matter, energy, time, and space at Yank-a-Pee Stadium to return to peace and harmony at once! I repeat. By the powers invested in me by Lord Metatron, Lord Melchizedek, Lord Ashtar, Lord Kumara, and Lord Maitreya, I command all matter, energy, time, and space at Yank-a-Pee Stadium to return to peace and harmony at once!

3RD BASE UMPIRE. Begging your pardon, Lord Buddha; it's *Yankee* Stadium.

BUDDHA. I *said* that.

And then by some strange incomprehensible alchemy unknown to mortal man, the mood at Yankee Stadium suddenly did a 180. The violence, melee, and confusion on the field and in the stands quickly dissipated and disappeared into thin air and all the ballplayers calmly went back to their respective positions and prepared to play ball again.

LADY. *Dang.* I was kickin' some Dandy ass then Buddha had to ruin everything with a peace party.

JOE. What strange alchemy is *this???* Things have really settled down here at Yankee Stadium.

TONY. They sure have Joe and it looks like we're about to play ball again.

Mr. Man takes a quick sip of chardonnay, steps back into the batter's box, takes a few check swings, and we're ready to go.

JOE. Clemens gets the sign from Posada and goes into his windup. Here's the pitch. High. Ball three.

TONY. Good eye by Mr. Man. That ball was just barely out of the strike zone. Mr. Man clearly waiting on a pitch he can hit outta the park.

JOE. The count is now 3 and 2 to Mr. Man. Clemens goes into his next windup. Here's the pitch ...

Clack ! ! ! Thump ! ! !

JOE. Fouled off of the plate. Just got a piece of it.

TONY. Mr. Man hanging on by a thread here in the bottom of the ninth.

JOE. Ready to go again. Clemens takes the sign from Posada. Here's the pitch ...

Crack ! ! ! Clack ! ! ! Thump ! ! ! Boom ! ! !

JOE. Mr. Man is down!!! Mr. Man is down and down *hard* at home plate!!!

TONY. He fouled the ball off his ankle.

JOE. That's the most painful thing in baseball. It's like getting hit by a sledgehammer.

TONY. Mr. Man struggling to get back on his feet.

JOE. He's back on his feet but he looks pretty bad off.

The TV crew zooms in on Mr. Man's ankle.

TONY. His ankle is bleeding, Joe.

JOE. That's not good.

TONY. It's doubtful Mr. Man will be able to continue the game.

JOE. That would be an automatic win for Clemens.

TONY. Home plate umpire Ed Montague walks over to Mr. Man to inspect the injury.

JOE. And Mr. Man walks away!!!

TONY. He doesn't wanna be taken out of the game.

JOE. He may not have a choice.

TONY. Montague reaches Mr. Man and points down at the ankle.

JOE. Mr. Man waves him off, says he's alright.

TONY. Montague points down at the bloody ankle again.

JOE. Mr. Man waves him off again. Says he's fine.

TONY. Montague shakes his head and continues to point at the ankle.

JOE. Mr. Man points at Lady in the dugout.

TONY. Montague shakes his head again and points at the bloody ankle.

JOE. Mr. Man shakes his head and points at Lady in the dugout.

TONY. We got a stand-off, Joe.

JOE. And now Clemens is hollering "Play Ball!!!"

And now the Yankee crowd gets into the act chanting,

Play Ball ! ! !   Play Ball ! ! !   Play Ball ! ! !

Play Ball ! ! !   Play Ball ! ! !   Play Ball ! ! !

Play Ball ! ! !   Play Ball ! ! !   Play Ball ! ! !

JOE. Holy mackerel! Ed Montague is getting pressured from three sides: Mr. Man, Clemens, and the Yankee crowd!

TONY. A lot is riding on Montague's decision. What's he gonna do???

Play Ball ! ! !   Play Ball ! ! !   Play Ball ! ! !

Play Ball ! ! !   Play Ball ! ! !   Play Ball ! ! !

Play Ball ! ! !   Play Ball ! ! !   Play Ball ! ! !

JOE. Montague throws up his hands!!! He's gonna let Mr. Man bat!!!

The Crowd Goes Wild ! ! !

JOE. Mr. Man limps slowly back into the batter's box.

TONY. He's in a lot of pain, Joe.

JOE. He sure is. What a trooper. He's given' this game his all.

TONY. Very tense moment here at Yankee Stadium.

JOE. Count remains 3 and 2 to Mr. Man. Clemens goes into his windup. Here's the pitch . . .

CRACK!!!

JOE. Towering blast deep center field!!! Way back!!! Way back!!! Williams is at the warning track!!! He's at the wall!!! It's *GONE!!!* Grand slam Mr. Man!!! Holy Toledo!!! Grand slam Mr. Man!!!

Lady Le Mans charges out of the dugout and begins clawing the shit out of home plate.

PLATE UMPIRE. Stop *that* Miss Lady!!! Home plate of Yankee Stadium is sacred!!! It is *not* a cat scratch pad!!!

LADY. It is *now!!!*

An eerie silence envelops Yankee Stadium as 38,374 dumbfounded Yankee fans look on in disbelief as their precious New York Yankees have just been beaten by some homeless dude and his cat.

Mr. Man hobbles around the bases and exchanges victorious fist bumps with Buddha, Freud, and the Professor at home plate, then Mr. Man scoops Lady up in his arms and they all walk slowly toward the locker room.

JOE. Holy mackerel! What a finish!

TONY. You said it, Joe. This is a game they'll be talking about for a long, long, time.

Inside the visitors locker room . . .

MR. MAN. I couldn't have done it without you guys.

BUDDHA. You learn fast Grasshopper. See you at OMA.

Buddha flashes Mr. Man a peace sign, then walks through a point in the wall and disappears.

Freud pulls out a match and lights a new cigar.

FREUD. Thursday. 2 O'clock.

MR. MAN. I'll be there.

A dreamy cloud of smoke bellows out of Freud's month and Freud walks through the same point in the wall and disappears.

The Professor smiles at Mr. Man.

PROFESSOR. Tat Tvam Asi.

MR. MAN. Tat Tvam Asi.

The Professor briskly taps his walking on the floor, then walks through the same point in the wall and disappears.

A few minutes later Mr. Man and Lady sit quietly in the car.

LADY. How's your ankle Mr. Man???

MR. MAN. I'll live.

LADY. You sure showed Clempsen.

MR. MAN. *Clemens.*

LADY. I said that.

MR. MAN. I saw you and Dandy goin' at it.

LADY. Yeah. Dandy's butt's gonna be sore tomorrow. That's for damn sure.

MR. MAN. It's you and me against the world Lady.

> *Lady gazes out the window.*

LADY. Poor world.

Mr. Man fires up "The Black Bat" and Mr. Man and Lady drive off into the night toward an uncertain future and more perilous adventures . . .

Mr. Man thinks he rescued me 19 years ago and I let him believe that. Of course, you and I both know it was I who rescued him 19 years ago. And all I've ever asked for in return is a little food and a warm bed. That's just the way I roll. I'm Lady Le Mans. And this is the end of the ride.

The fundamental building block of reality is MAGIC and probability waves inform us 750 trillion times per second that anything is possible. I oughta know. I wrote this entire book living in a car with a cat on a borrowed computer.

It is done Professor.

Z. Z. LE MANS

Public Parking Garage
December 25, 2023

Special Thanks

José Garcia

Mel Raven

Dr. Griesshaber

Kurtis Switzer

John Freeman

Kim Freeman

Robert Bright

Buck Johnson

Image Credits

Front Cover...(design) Z. Z. Le Mans (artist) Mikey Tabarcea
Z. Z. & Lady Le Mans (all)...Z. Z. Le Mans
Catholic Nun..houstonchronicle.com
Vacant Lot Baseball...texascooppower.com
Joe Garagiola & Tony Kubek...thespitter.com
High School...amle.org
Phil Wood & Company...fatlace.com
Buddha..quora.com
De Anza College...dreamstudiesabroad.com
Shattered Dreams..wordpress.com
Fall into Addiction...fernandarubio.com
The Black Bat (all)..Z. Z. Le Mans
Paul & Eddie's ....Z. Z. Le Mans
Black Berry Farm sign...Z. Z. Le Mans
Freud (page 66)...neuronsnotincluded.com
Kim Freeman...lostcatfinder.com
Night Walker...depositphotos.com
Front Door Key Lock...seattletimes.com
Doppelganger Cats...sinogene.org
Judith West..Z. Z. Le Mans
Elk Brand Crate Label...the labelman.com
Ed Travaras...Phil Nelson, Cupertino Courier
Welcome to Stanford...stanfordreview.org
The Two Paths..okolonacc.org
The Grady Twins..theshining.fandom.com
Redrum...gifer.com
Haunted House..unsplash.com
Freud (page 106) .... brown.edu
Litter Box...amazon.com
Dumpster..artstation.com
Dumpster Demon..undeadwalking.com
Cosmic Octopus...nypost.com
Quantum Entanglement Equation....................................scitechdaily.com
Niels Bohr...ifunny.com
Porta Potty...Z. Z. Le Mans
Dome of Destiny..theatlantic.com
Theodore Roosevelt...twitter.com
Skateboard Headstone...dribbble.com
Typewriter & Scotch ....planetsmag.com
Busted Again ....thinkaloud.net
Yankee Stadium...unityig.com
Roger Clemens (all)...pinstripealley.com
Dandy...nypost.com
All Other Images...pinterest.com

24" x 34" Gallery Quality Fine Art Print
inprnt.com/gallery/prints

Printed in the USA
CPSIA information can be obtained
at www.ICGtesting.com
CBHW020355041024
15321CB00056B/1913

9 781088 030981